KITCHEN CON

KITCHEN CON

WRITING ON THE RESTAURANT RACKET

TREVOR WHITE

Including a conversation with
ANTHONY BOURDAIN

**ARCADE
PUBLISHING**

First published in the United Kingdom by Mainstream Publishing.

Arcade Publishing books may be purchased in bulk at special discounts for sales promotion, corporate gifts, fund-raising, or educational purposes. Special editions can also be created to specifications. For details, contact the Special Sales Department, Arcade Publishing, 307 West 36th Street, 11th Floor, New York, NY 10018 or arcade@skyhorsepublishing.com.

Arcade Publishing® is a registered trademark of Skyhorse Publishing, Inc.®, a Delaware corporation.

Visit our website at www.arcadepub.com.

10 9 8 7 6 5 4 3 2 1

Library of Congress Cataloging-in-Publication Data is available on file.

ISBN: 978-1-61145-465-9

Printed in the United States of America

For Peter and Alicia White

A critic's job, nine-tenths of it, is to make way
for the good by demolishing the bad.

—Kenneth Tynan

Contents

Introduction

This is a book about dining out, which begins with a reservation: the restaurant business is more accurately described as a racket. That reservation will not guarantee a table anywhere, much less a warm reception. However, it is made — or muttered — whenever humans eat in public. Until quite recently, most normal people were reluctant to dress up, endure rude service, and pay for food that was sometimes fatal and always expensive. There was probably a difference between the scams of the culinary cartel and the antics of convicted criminals, but no one was quite sure what it was, so everyone practiced caution. "In restaurants," says the novelist Martin Amis, "my father always wore an air of vigilance, as if in expectation of being patronised, stiffed, neglected, or regaled by pretension."

Today, eating out is a part of the life well lived. Restaurants are a destination, and we go in greater numbers than ever before. Encouraged to believe that no one has time to cook anymore, we fling ourselves at much-hyped chefs like a nation of hungry sheep. The dining room, a place where people once came to parse the news, has now become the news itself. So the fact that entrees in some New York restaurants now cost more than $40 is not mere marginalia. It makes the front page of the *New York Times.*

The blame, or the credit, does not lie solely with the media. We read more menus than recipes for many reasons, including the most banal: the demise of the traditional family, sexual liberation, more disposable income, TV, snobbery, cheap airfares, and the eclecticism that travel encourages. This is reflected in the sort of menus that offer smoked eel, pad thai, and pepper ice cream. (If that strikes you as a ridiculous mixture, you are not conceited enough to work in a professional kitchen, where the vile frequently masquerades as the exotic.)

The burgeoning popularity of restaurants is largely a positive phenomenon. However, when they're not just bemused, diners have a right to feel short-changed. Some restaurants are owned by thieves. Others are staffed by the criminally insane. All are reviewed by the sort of people who believe that no good meal is complete without a sorbet to cleanse the palate, and that Michelin stars keep the sky from falling down.

Later in this book, I will look at the history of restaurant criticism, as well as some of the loudest voices in the racket today. Many have catching up to do. In Britain, this means admitting that London is another country. In America, it means acknowledging that people dine out for a variety of reasons, and, often, the food is incidental. And while newspapers focus on celebrity chefs, the real news in restaurants is at the other end of the market. Slapdash dining is what most customers want, which explains the rise of the dreaded taco and the all-weather smile of a clown called Ronald McDonald.

As a restaurant critic, I am conscious of the position that my colleagues now occupy in the culture. There are 40,000 restaurants in the United States, and Americans spend 49 cents of every food dollar on food eaten outside the home. In other words, half the nation's provender is now consumed in public. As we choose to dine out more often, the power of the press increases. Critics deny that they have the power to close a restaurant. They can certainly make a chef, a fact that lends the activity cachet. Like politicians' wives — unaccountable, powerful, and usually up to mischief — they have almost emerged by stealth. Some are invidious, many are pompous, and the job itself is not exactly onerous. Yet the best provide a public service.

In an age that feels almost fatally harried, good restaurants are where we relax in the company of people we like, where we remove ourselves from what goes on outside, elsewhere, somewhere not this civil. They are where we try new flavors, where we feel pampered or rewarded and where we connect with people who are important to us. Under the right circumstances — and pointed in the right direction — the dining room is a place in which we become some slightly more attractive version of ourselves.

In addition to exploring how humans eat in public, this book contains the confession of a small-town hack. Social history gives way, in parts, to memoir; elsewhere the reader is offered practical advice on how to get the best out of restaurants. The book, which took three years to write, charts a journey of sorts — throughout, my view of lunch may be no clearer than your own. I grew up in Ireland, where my parents owned a famous restaurant, at a time when the recipe for mashed potatoes was still regarded as a national treasure. To this day, there is only one way in which I might be described as a culinary expert: I love spaghetti westerns.

You may well wonder why the gaps in my knowledge have not been exposed before. You may also discover how easy it is to become a judge of dinner. All you need is a pen, some paper, and an appetite. Restaurants are in business to offer a service, and if you pay for that service, you're entitled to have an opinion. As long as you don't break the law, you are also free to share it. These are the rules of the new restaurant criticism, and of something grander still: democracy. *Kitchen Con* tries to determine what this means for customer, critic, and chef.

Finally, this book lauds a breathtaking display of consumer democracy. Few commentators have championed the event in print, and with good reason: it poses an unprecedented threat to critic and chef alike. They are the people who traditionally decide what good taste means. But the rise of the Internet is changing the game forever, as thousands of sites emerge to lend all diners a voice. In other words, the customer is becoming the critic.

That knowledge is exciting. Like dinner tonight, it comes at a price and prompts new speculation. Is it fair to feast while others starve? Why are waiters like cocaine dealers? Can one ever trust a guidebook? Is it lawful to leave a restaurant without paying? And which fool picked that wallpaper?

To answer those questions, join me for dinner in London, Paris, and New York. Along the way, we shall meet great guardians of gastronomy, each choking on a slab of foie gras. A few may survive, but it won't be pretty — and where we're going, those Michelin stars mean nothing. It's not that sort of place.

Welcome to the Twenty-First-Century Dining Room.

Part One

1

The Hungry Hooker

Why Restaurants Are Brothels for the Mouth

IN 1998, OSAMA BIN LADEN MET AND IMPRISONED A WOMAN CALLED Kola Boof. Then he forced her to have sex. A lot. "He loves infidels," she said, "as long as they're pretty women from the Western world. He likes to beat them." Six months later, the world's most wanted Muslim ran off with a Jewish stripper.

Kola Boof was later exposed as a prostitute.

These events took place in La Maison Arabe. I was there in the autumn of 2003, reviewing it for a French magazine. Calm and comfortable, this small hotel is where the jet set stay in Marrakech. Guests play backgammon in the evening, everyone speaks three languages — and Kola Boof loves the orange sponge cake. La Maison Arabe is elegant, but difficult to review, for the hotel has acquired a reputation that no amount of praise will shift.

I could have ignored the Kola Boof connection. Then, however, I would not have had a story. A journalist without a story is like a chef without a temper. So I told the truth, got my story, and heaped further notoriety on a beautiful place. I didn't feel comfortable about the article, but I also knew that the repercussions would probably not be grave. It was all so far away.

Two weeks later, I was asked to review a restaurant in Connemara for an Irish newspaper. "It's important," said the editor, "to know what Dubliners eat on holiday."

A small fishing village on the western edge of Europe, Roundstone is where the new rich go to act like simple peasant folk. On the day I arrived, the village was full of big-smoke lawyers letting off steam. Their voices were conspicuous, unashamedly metropolitan. Travelers, not tourists — only they *were* tourists: rich sucker tourists. I had lunch and dinner in O'Dowd's pub and restaurant for four consecutive days. There, judgment was passed on constitutional amendments, Keith Floyd, and the size of the ass on Jennifer Lopez. I was struck by the fact that middle-aged men look ludicrous in jeans. The food was indescribable. What could I say about the spicy chicken wings in a barbecue sauce? Nothing. The chicken Kiev with coleslaw? Please. The famous seafood chowder?

Any assessment of the menu would imply that it warranted sober analysis.

I had hesitated to shaft La Maison Arabe; and then I'd gone to work. O'Dowd's was different, closer, somehow more personal. To shaft a pub in a seaside village, I would probably upset a lot of friends. Better, perhaps, to fake satisfaction. What greater cause would a bad review serve? The notion that one person's opinion on the matter could be useful to another person suddenly struck me as ridiculous. And to suggest that the opinion might be objective — whatever that means — seemed even more silly. I was trying to worm my way out of a tight spot; made no effort to hide that fact. But evasion prompted further, unwelcome reflection.

The charade of solemnity now felt impertinent. Starvation is a culinary issue. So, too, is the price of dinner. Does it really matter if the dreams of the bourgeoisie are realized? And if it does, why is the system for encouraging greatness so inept? People become restaurant critics in the hope that they can impress friends, influence strangers, and secure reservations at places where other people routinely contract salmonella. Few discuss the fraudulence at the heart of the racket, and no one has ever explored it in a book. No critic has any credentials, beyond some nebulous love of food. There is no manual in which instructions are provided. Critical styles are not analyzed, nor trends assessed. In fact, all one can say with any certainty about people who review the food in restaurants is that (a) diners envy them, (b) chefs hate them, and (c) they usually work undercover.

None of that seemed like useful information. After ten years working as a restaurant critic — ten quietly comfortable years — one shit pub provoked a crisis.

Here are the rest of my thoughts on the afternoon of November 3, 2003:

> I feel sorry for the man who owns this place. He was kind enough to make me tea this morning, when the pub wasn't even open.
> That smell in the men's.
> I have eaten here eight times in four days. Neither they nor I have any excuse.
> You could write it as a color piece. Lots of dialogue, very little description.
> That wouldn't be a restaurant review.

What is a critic supposed to do when the food is not worth discussing and the rent still demands to be paid? Tell the truth. Right? If critics serve truth, we must admit its contradictions. I could recommend this village, but not without noting that its famous restaurant is better at being a pub and the locals are *anything but local*. That's what I told my editor. She didn't buy it. So I wrote an account of the week. I was trying to share misgivings, not some culinary scandal.

"It's OK," said the editor. "But you didn't mention the food."

"The food?" I asked. "Who cares about the food?"

"Everyone," she said. "It's what readers want to know."

"You know, I used to think that too."

"What do you mean?"

"*Who cares* what some stranger had for dinner last night?"

"It's what critics do."

"Oh, like part of a ritual?"

"Yes, part of a ritual that people did long before *you* came along."

"It's a racket," I said. "Crooked to the bone. There's no such thing as a truly impartial hack, and there's no such thing as a gourmet critic. On some level, *everyone* is bluffing."

"The least you can do is try."

"Can I predict what sort of experience you're going to have in a restaurant that I've been to once, twice, even a dozen times? I'm a critic; of course they're going to spoil me. Why pretend that we're ordinary customers? And what's the difference anyway?"

"Now you're contradicting yourself."

"Good critics don't give a damn about objectivity. Chefs hate them for daring to admit that there's more to dining than dinner itself, and the public lap it up. I say we write for diners, not the vanity of chefs. It's those same diners, by the way, who are snapping at our heels. They're the real opinion-formers. And to answer your question, the reason why I don't write about the food is because most of the time it's not worth mentioning."

"But you're supposed to be a food critic!"

"No. I'm a *restaurant* critic."

"Look," she said. "Write the story."

In telling this tale of a critic who choked — it started with a woman who may, or may not, have been a prostitute — I have often felt like a grand impostor. Nobody knew what Kola Boof was doing in Marrakech. Am I anything more than a hungry hooker? Reviewers are hired to masquerade as people who can't say no. We are paid to do what others consider a pleasure, and then declare ourselves disgusted.

Critics work under exceptional circumstances, yet these are peculiar times for all journalists. One of our functions is to unmask corruption. Widely regarded as a lavish scam, pursued by verbose con men, the profession itself has never been under more attack. And there is, of course, something of the mercenary about all authors. The comedian Lenny Bruce used to do a routine about a traveling salesman who checked into a hotel and called down from his room for a hundred-dollar prostitute. "A few minutes later," said Bruce, "there's a knock on the door, and a bearded writer comes into the room."

That story is cute, but the hooker thing doesn't quite work. I want to look at the restaurant press in greater detail, and I want to look, too, at the Kitchen Con, to ask who, or what, that term describes. Both intentions require some context: how you eat, and why that matters. "Great restaurants," said the writer Frederic Raphael, "are nothing but brothels for the mouth." If that is true, then we each have a case to answer. In the Twenty-First-Century Dining Room, the critic and the chef are up to mischief, but the customer pays the bills. And this litany of misdeeds is not complete without reference to those who produce and sell the food that you're so keen to consume.

For what we're about to receive, someone ought to be locked up. But who?

"What in the world is that?"

2

The Age of Appetite

A Survey of the Way We Eat Today

I N THE PAST, HUMANS WERE OBLIGED TO PREPARE THEIR OWN FOOD and drink. We know, for instance, that during World War II, every Italian soldier in North Africa carried an espresso machine. Most homes in the rich world now have a kitchen complete with oven, sink, and fridge of regulation width. The room is purpose-built and well equipped for baking, boiling, and frying. We occasionally do all three. Most of the time, we're out to dinner, at that new Italian round the corner. That may be just as well. For the food we consume at home is liable to kill us soon enough.

In this short survey of the way that food is produced, consumed, and judged, it will be observed that humans are abandoning the kitchen, that Jamie Oliver is a touchstone in this regard (for reasons he must resent), and that anyone who knows how to hold a pen could now work as a restaurant critic. At the end of this chapter, you may wish to voice your disgust in public, or you may never want to eat again. That would be quite understandable. In the Age of Appetite, the business of dinner is complex, trivial, glamorous, and depressing. Indeed, one might well start by asking: Why do we bother to eat at all?

Why Do We Eat?

We eat to fuel, or refuel, the body. A meal can please us, briefly, and the sight of a full larder encourages the fantasy that we are in control of the planet. On the day he was found in a hole, Saddam Hussein was hoarding $750,000, some chickens, and "several" Bounty bars. Food fuels the mind (nothing tastes as good as that which one has never eaten) and food is an instrument of social one-upmanship. The new name-droppers are people who order off the menu, and it is possible to be more ostentatious still. When a friend of mine said, "I didn't know anything about good cooking until I had real bouillabaisse in Juan les Pins," what she meant was, "I can afford to go to the south of France."

Dr. Steven Shapin lectures on the history of science at Harvard. He also writes about food for the *New Yorker*. That is where I found this succinct analysis of the relationship between food and self-image:

> A temperate person is someone who eats temperately; a posh and powerful person is someone who gets an eight o'clock table at The Ivy; respect for life is shown by vegetarianism; red-blooded machismo by the consumption of red meat; your friends eat with you at home; the High eat later than the Low, thus making a standard display of delayed gratification and acquiring the associated status of those who can wait an hour longer than others for their food. Self-nourishing and self-fashioning both happen at the table.

Vegetarians: Are They Safe to Eat?

Vegetarians are the lesbians of the food world. Misunderstood, widely maligned, and constantly screaming oppression, they are never accused of wearing difference lightly. Most are regarded as interlopers by purists. If you eat fish, you are a pescetarian. If you eat plants that are picked without killing the host, such as avocados and tomatoes, you are a fruitarian, but not necessarily a raw foodist, who eats everything raw to pre-serve the enzymes. Most raw foodists are children of people who drive Range Rovers with leather seats and tinted windows; they talk of nothing but nuts, seeds, and Balinese retreats, and their favorite verb is "purge."

Millions of humans have died because of food, be it stale or poisonous. Yet more have died for the want of food. We have a moral obligation to meet this disgrace with valor. Some people think that becoming a vegetarian is an honorable way to acknowledge a degree of personal responsibility for global inequality. They point out that by the year 2050, livestock will require the equivalent amount of land and water as four billion humans: do we feed the world, or feed our livestock? But there are sound arguments against vegetarianism. Any group that pursues its own interests has an impact on the rest of the natural kingdom, and even if we all became vegetarians, domes-ticated meat species would not simply return to the wild.

"We must not shirk the moral dimension in our dealings with meat," argues Hugh Fearnley-Whittingstall, a champion of dead cow. That means raising and killing animals without cruelty, and do-ing them the respect of eating every last bit, from pigs' ears to slow-braised oxtails. If that sounds gruesome, go vegetarian. My girlfriend was a pescetarian until she was tempted by a 12-ounce steak at her thirtieth birthday dinner. We raised a glass to new departures, and I felt almost smug, as if her defection represented a moral victory for omnivores. It does not, no more than a crash is good for other cars.

Perhaps we should encourage vegetarians: both moral and self-ish, this position has the twin benefits of serving a greater good and ensuring that there is a plentiful supply of meat for the rest of us. (Woody Harrelson — you the man.) The consumption of sirloin steak may well be indefensible. The pleasure is incomparable.

Cooking is a source of cliché, and also of metaphor. The word "sweet" was one of Shakespeare's favorite modifiers, while a genre of food-writing argues that there is no better way to discuss people than to talk about what we eat. Best-selling books on cod, cheese, and coffee claim that a knowledge of their history increases our understanding of the human condition. Sometimes, however, food-as-metaphor is advanced with rather too much ickiness. *Chocolat* may be the second-worst film of all time.

Food is a weapon. In Zimbabwe, once known as the breadbasket of Africa, a senior member of the opposition recently said, "The banning of foreign feeding programs means that the government controls all food. The clear message is: either you vote the right way or you and your children will starve." Sometimes that starvation is self-inflicted: fasting has long been a political and religious tool, providing time, as Shapin notes, to mobilize public sentiment.

Eating alone can sometimes feel like a privilege. Eating together can encourage goodwill and companionship. Professor Robert Putnam, the man who promoted the term social capital (referring to the number and quality of our connections with other people), says people are withdrawing from communal life, choosing instead to live alone and play alone. We are in danger, he warns, of becoming mere observers of our collective destiny. "Certainly in writing *Bowling Alone,*" Putnam told me, "I was very struck by the way in which eating is at the center of social capital, from dinner parties to picnics to family dinners."

Putnam is big on third places, those locations that are neither home nor work. Among his ideas for increasing the stock of social capital in a community, he suggested a designated meet-people table, as there are in some clubs and, increasingly, in restaurants such as New York's Buddakan and Mercer Kitchen. One might devote a large round table to walk-in business: ask diners who haven't reserved if they would share that table with strangers. Assign it, perhaps, to customers on a budget, and offer a cheap, set menu on that table alone.

Finally, as Steven Shapin writes, eating is a moment of ontological transformation, complete with religious undertones and social implications:

> It is when what is not you — not rational and not animate, at the time you consume it — starts to become you, the rational being

which ultimately decides what stuff to consume. Flesh becomes reason at one remove, and every supper is, in that sense, Eucharistic. We are, literally and fundamentally, what we eat.

Your Life on a Plate

If we are what we eat, that is a pity, for the food we consume at home is literally and fundamentally shocking. In Britain, sales of heavily processed foods — instant korma, microwave lasagna — trebled between 1992 and 2002. There, consumers spend £7,000 ($14,000) a minute on "wholesome," "traditional," and "homemade" treats that contain enough chemicals to slay a weaker beast. Encouraged by a powerful, well-funded food industry — in America, $36 billion is spent on marketing food every year — we are eating more junk food than ever. "The food industry must compete fiercely for every dollar spent on food," explains the food scientist Marion Nestle, "and food companies expend extraordinary resources to develop and market products that will sell, regardless of their effect on nutritional status or waistlines."

Until recently, our corpses started to rot in three days. Now it takes three weeks because of the preservatives that line our dead bodies. The margin on processed foods with a long shelf life is much greater than it is on "old-fashioned" foods. Processed foods are cheaper at the checkout — and there alone — which helps to explain why supermarket aisles are stacked high with stuff that one should not really eat. In 1978, 8 percent of American homes had microwave ovens. Today? Eighty-three percent. It is still possible to buy fruit and vegetables in supermarkets. Bred for consistency and appearance, they sparkle (at regulation size) and have never tasted quite so bland.

In 2006, *New York* magazine ran a story on the Hybrid Round Red, a tomato grown on a 17,000-acre Pacific Tomato Growers megafarm in Florida, crossbred with other varieties to thwart ailments such as Alternaria stem canker. The soil's pH is adjusted, nitrogen, phosphorus, and potassium are added, and the plant is fumigated with pesticide to repel insects. The journey continues:

> To simplify packing, the tomato is plucked from the vine before it's ripe, as a stage called "mature green" — fully grown but with the texture closer to an apple — and emptied into a vast "gondola" before washing and sorting. From there, the tomato heads by truck to a packing plant, where it receives a disinfecting chlorinated bath, a cooldown (a mature green tomato can chill for two weeks at 58 degrees Fahrenheit without any noticeable consequences), and a stay in the ripening room, a chamber filled with ethylene, which turns tomatoes the desired sunset shade.
>
> Finally, Red is sorted for size, eyeballed for imperfections, slicked with food-grade vegetable wax (making it glossy and impervious to the bumpy ride ahead), and piled into a twenty-five-pound ventilated carton. After a two-day, 1,250 mile journey, it arrives at a New York supermarket, where it can sit for a week without any change in texture or taste, such as it is.

It should not be assumed that government is doing a whole lot to guarantee a measure of quality in the food chain. In many countries, subsidies support the production of fats, starches, and sweeteners, the raw materials of the food-processing industry.

The meat racket isn't much better. To maximize profits, animals are kept in spaces so small that they can hardly move. With nowhere to go, they don't grow normally. To fatten them up, farmers pump cows with anabolic steroids, growth hormones, and beta-agonists. If you feel a bit jumpy after your next steak, don't be too surprised: beta-agonists can cause heart tremors. And if you think a lot of meat tastes as if it has been marinated in its own blood, give yourself a clap on the back. You're right. Before you express your disgust, however, make sure you're well within your rights. As Oprah Winfrey learned when she dared to question the quality of American beef, there is no defaming steak in certain states. Food can sue you now.

Ask a young person how to boil an egg. Observe the creases that line the forehead, the mild shrug of the shoulders, and the mouth agape. The Good Food Foundation has discovered that most eight- to fourteen-year-olds are capable of adding milk to cereal and making a sandwich. That's all. Another survey reveals that 69 percent of British three-year-olds can identify the golden arches, but half of four-year-olds do not know their own name. The situation is more alarming still in the United States, with its meals on wheels for the rich. Every night, thousands of deliverymen cycle the streets of Manhattan, bearing restaurant food for children whose parents are too busy or drowsy to heat a bowl of soup. If the doorbell rings after seven o'clock, those same kids — spoiled, or neglected — start a Pavlovian chant of "Dinner!"

The Rise of the Restaurant

That mild shrug of the shoulders is not confined to children. Never have people been so interested in food and so disinclined to cook. Thus we talk with authority about the best chef in town — as if it was part of our job — and we don't know how to season a stew. Food writer Molly O'Neill has discovered that the less Americans cook, the more they spend on cooking appliances. A 2005 survey reveals that the following are "typical attitudes" of twenty-six- to fifty-year-old consumers:

> "I get home late and I want to sit down with a glass of wine and eat something that will be ready in five minutes. Cooking isn't a pleasure. Eating is."
> "I don't go to dinner parties. My friends simply don't have them any more. We'll go out to a restaurant, or meet for drinks in a bar."
> "I go out every evening after work, and the only thing I can cook is pasta with tomato sauce. But I love new restaurants."

After reviewing the statistics, the trends, the enduring truths and the new discoveries, one is left with a picture of the modern human that looks something like this:

We are not healthy or patient.
We are hungry, lazy, and going to have the special.★

Longer working hours and the pace of modern life are often suggested as reasons for eating on the hoof. Sociologists tell us that express lanes in fast-food joints illustrate the fact that we are all under great pressure. Yet many of the people who spend a lot of time in restaurants have a truly embarrassing amount of freedom.

Woody Allen dines out every night for the same reason that he makes a new film every year. "What else would I do?" says Allen. "Life is a meaningless grind . . . There's plenty of time to do all this stuff." In that regard, at least, Allen is not unique. In his book *Urban Tribes,* Ethan Watters chronicles the lives of his overeducated, single, unmortgaged, urban, thirty-something peer group. The sort of characters one meets in a Wes Anderson movie, they work in Starbucks — not serving coffee, but writing a screenplay. Still. Struggling authors and the great set pieces — from proposal to end of affair — share a stage in the Twenty-First-Century Dining Room.

"We were not tied down by family," writes Watters. "We had remarkable freedom in how we pursued romantic relationships; we were free from general strife and the thinking of some national movement or other . . . and, most significantly, we had the freedom of time."

How, then, should one celebrate all this freedom?

"Dine we must," said Mrs. Beeton, who died at the age of twenty-eight, "and we may as well dine elegantly as well as wholesomely." Eager to impress, millions now follow her advice. We meet lovers, flatter seniors, suffer bores, and get jobs in the Twenty-First-Century Dining Room. We go to make money, and to spend it, and we go in times of

---

★This synopsis may not do justice to the species. It has been noted, for instance, that we are also more pretentious than flamingos. That is why we clamor for tables at Gramercy Tavern and gawk at minor celebrities in the toilet. There's a *New Yorker* cartoon in which a man gets into a cab, shouting to the driver: "And step on it. This restaurant may be over any minute." Affectation explains why we boast to strangers on the phone ("I'm a friend of the owner") and why we dress up to go out for a pizza.

plenty — sorrow, too. The most memorable meal of my life was lunch, after a funeral, in the function room of a suburban golf club. I can still see the drizzle on the eighteenth green.

Life can end in restaurants — opening an oyster is never so impressive as the Heimlich maneuver — just as another begins. "Yes, it was five minutes of small talk," recalls Boris Becker, "then into the nearest suitable corner for our business." That little conclave led to the birth of a daughter and the end of a marriage. Even by the standards of an aging tennis player, the choice of venue was not particularly intelligent. There are no quiet corners in Nobu.

The restaurant menu is a relatively new invention. Its history is a tale, often told in French, of fits, spurts, and occasional mushrooms. In 1915, there were 8,000 restaurants in the city of New York. Ten years later, there were 17,000. In 1960, there were three Vietnamese restaurants in Paris. Today, there are more than 6,000. Last year, 300,000 people tried to make a reservation at one Spanish restaurant, El Bulli. Eight thousand succeeded. Residents of twelve American cities now eat more food cooked by strangers than by themselves or people they know.

Our ancestors were often more concerned with the quantity of food available to them than the quality. Today, we are spoiled *by* choice, and in living well — too well, sometimes — we can't get enough of the new. One used to say exotic, but the word has lost all meaning. Heston Blumenthal started cooking for the English public eleven years ago. In 2005, The Fat Duck, his restaurant in Berkshire, was fêted as the best in the world by *Restaurant* magazine, and "The Wizard of Odd" has three Michelin stars for a menu that is full of freak-show food such as smoky-bacon ice cream and snail porridge. When Rita Dalmia opened Diva, Delhi's top Italian restaurant, customers would send back al dente risotto because they were used to very soft basmati rice. Not anymore. In a recent six-month period, Rashmi Uday Singh reviewed Korean, Moroccan, Malaysian, Indonesian, Italian, Lebanese, Burmese, and Mongolian restaurants in Mumbai. "The growing middle-class double-income families have more disposable income," she told a newspaper in 2005. "They travel, have access to cable television and the Internet. All this has led to more exposure of the palate to the outside world."

Food as Fashion

"Chocolate is the next coffee."
— *New York Times*

"Fish is the new steak."
— *The Times*

"Chocolate is the new olive oil."
— *New York Times*

"Wheatgrass is the new cocaine."
— *The Times*

"Chocolate is the new fruit."
— *The Independent*

"Wheatgrass is the new carrot juice."
— *Daily Mail*

"Chickpeas should be the new baked beans!"
— *The Express*

Diners have a voracious appetite for culinary titbits, which make gastronomy sound like showbiz. Restaurateurs do not work in the catering industry. They are impresarios. And culinary tourism has replaced the theater with nights at Babbo and Jean Georges. Even the battle of the bulge is chic: star loses weight on hip new diet; millions want to know her secret; star gets rich on fat of the land.

Atkins Mania

The Atkins diet deserves special mention among thousands of quick-fix remedies for pants that keep getting smaller. The *New Diet Revolution* spawned a $30-billion market for low-carbohydrate cookbooks, foods, and assorted paraphernalia. The fundamental tenets of this secular religion mirror the salvation story of the Bible. A challenge is set down to all converts, who must fight the forces of evil — the people who gave you carb-addiction — and adhere to a life-changing regimen, complete with Commandments and a radical denunciation of received wisdom. An early antipathy to big business was later toned down as the company behind it became vastly profitable, aligning Atkins with the organic and Slow Food movements. ("When I eat a slice of ham, it becomes part of me," said Carlo Petrini, the founder of Slow Food. "That's why I spend money on food.") Thirty million Americans — Generation XXL — decided to give the diet a go. When Dr. Atkins died at the age of seventy-two, after slipping on a New York pavement, he was reported to be clinically obese.

The Oliver Twist

Dieting is big business. So is gorging. About 600 million books on cooking and wine are bought by Americans each year. In 2002, 4,000 hours of cooking programs were shown on British television, and the Food Network now broadcasts into 90 million American homes. We celebrate those who would show us how to cook, even if we don't always want to learn. And while the subject has never been sexier (gastro-porn), many of us are mere observers (culinary voyeurism). Sometimes, of course, it's nice to watch: witness the ability of Nigella Lawson to wet a man's lips without moving her own. "I am not a chef," says the Domestic Goddess. "I am not even a trained or professional cook. My qualification is as an eater."

London has also spawned the Justin Timberlake of TV dinners. Young, cute, and studiously raffish, Jamie Oliver opened a bistro in Hackney, staffed by unemployed kids who didn't know how to cook. It was the subject of a successful documentary series that deftly blended reality television with the game show and the cooking program. In 2005, Oliver presented another series on the subject of school dinners. As a result of what one commentator called "celebrity fairy dust" and another called "celebrity duress," the government agreed to invest an additional £45 ($90) million to improve the quality of meals in Britain's schools. Not a bad start for the Naked Chef, whose one-man assault on Turkey Twizzlers (a particularly unpleasant children's snack) could yet prove successful.

It is hard to fault Jamie Oliver's zeal — he currently sells 2.5 million cookbooks a year — but the chef has yet to convince his fans to spend much time in the kitchen. When the British food chain Sainsbury's, which has paid Oliver several million dollars to star in its advertisements, surveyed its customers in January 2006, 90 percent said they own a cookbook, but over half never use it. In the same survey, 75 percent of people said they eat the same food every week. (And it is delights like Sainsbury's farmed salmon that those same customers turn to when they do spend time in the kitchen. Oliver was recently described as "a whore" by fellow British TV chef Clarissa Dickson Wright after he endorsed the product, even though he refused to serve it.)

This confusion extends to the public image of a man who bills himself as a consumer champion. Department of Uncomfortable Truths: Jamie Oliver MBE is an icon for a lot of men and women who are fascinated by food and totally unwilling to cook. The fact that he shares a name with a boy who famously asked for more lends the following paradox greater punch:

The Oliver Twist: Eat more, cook less.

Diner Becomes Critic

Oliver's fans will resent that construction. Some may even express their outrage in print. If the question is "What's cooking?" the answer is "writing." A boom in restaurant culture, coupled with the deification of personal experience and the rise of new technology, has spawned a generation of amateur critics. It is almost as if everyone has been diagnosed with listeria, or shown, at least, to the same bad table by that dear little man in the dirty black shirt who thinks he's Graham Norton. Like Peter Finch in *Network,* we're mad as hell and we're not going to take it anymore.

Food rage has been a sociological phenomenon for several decades — a friend of mine is writing a thesis on it — but it only went mainstream after Michael Douglas had his egg-muffin moment in *Falling Down.* "Sorry," said the server, "it's ten thirty-three, and we don't do breakfast after ten thirty. You'll have to order off the lunch menu." At that point, Douglas produced a submachine gun. Was he right to resort to violence? Your answer depends on the sort of service you are used to receiving; what is inarguable is that customers have begun to fight back. The Internet has democratized an activity previously reserved for the self-styled elite, changing the nature of our relationship with restaurants, in a way that empowers consumers.

In the Age of Appetite, the diner has *become* the critic, and the critic had better take stock of the change. Much of the commentary on restaurant culture is now published on the Web, in a freewheeling manner that seems antithetical to the archaic conventions of gastronomy and criticism. Alongside the market leader, egullet.com, there are thousands of platforms for sharing gripes, good news, and reviews, with names that are even more exotic than some of the opinions expressed: Culinary Hags, Chile Fork, Noodle Pie, Mamster's Grub Shack, and Restaurant Whore, "A San Francisco Girl's Down and Dirty Guide to her Adventures in the Culinary Playground."

Everyone has, at some point, wanted to exact revenge on a chef. In the past, that was hard to do without a can of paint or a portable megaphone. Thanks to the Internet, revenge is suddenly sweet, sour, whatever you're having yourself. This is not to suggest, however, that the Web is the only place where criticism flourishes. In England, newspaper critics are even more vicious than their online rivals.

The Dogs of Dinner

Restaurant criticism is the only blood sport that liberals are allowed to like these days. In London, the dogs of dinner are not introduced but unleashed by editors; more concerned with entertaining diners than flattering cooks or regurgitating recipes, they rush like judge and jury, as if to the scene of a poisoning. All chefs are guilty until proven innocent, descriptions of the food often seem like an afterthought, there is little regard for gastronomic dogma or journalistic ethics, and, in one case, a reviewer has been hired with a specific brief to write about the food in just one paragraph, leaving lots of room for exhaustive descriptions of the scene.

We are witnessing a transfer of power in the restaurant racket, from the chef to the customer, who is often the critic. A lot of passionate amateurs and a gang of loudmouth hacks are changing the perception of restaurants within the culture. It is easy to hate these newcomers, which explains the failure of other journalists to acknowledge their achievements. When the service is poor, the lighting is too bright, or the font on the menu is not to their liking, *les rosbifs* scream of their suffering like an ungrateful child on Christmas Day.

A Burgeoning Market

Parents tell their children to be grateful for what they have. In Ireland, this is usually accompanied by a sermon on the Famine. Apparently there is no suffering like the old suffering. During the siege of Paris in 1870, restaurateurs were reduced to cooking animals from the zoo. On

Christmas Day, the menu at one famous brasserie included *consommé d'éléphant* and *le chat flanqué de rats*. The elephant soup was popular. History records no response to a plate of cat with rat. Today, our meals are all recorded, and you can get anything you want in a restaurant, from Afghan pot to Three-Shout Rat, something of a delicacy in China. Here are the instructions:

> Take a newborn rat between your chopsticks. It'll squeak.
> Dip it in strong alcohol; it'll squeak again and faint.
> Take a bite; it'll squeak again and die.

You need courage in the Twenty-First-Century Dining Room to endure a lot of dangerous nonsense. Food may lend spectacular joy to life, but most of the time it is shocking, bland, unhealthy, or expensive. We have more and more time and money to spend dining out, which we do with astonishing gusto, yet many pretend that the standard of cooking has improved in the home. Deceit is rife in the culinary world, from the true cost of processed food to the vanity of chefs who regard themselves as artists.

The self-deception implicit in the casting of Jamie Oliver as culinary savior is mirrored in the way that restaurateurs misrepresent the role of the media. A restaurant boom is seldom attributed to the prominence afforded the industry, while the correlation between frank reviews and better cooking is similarly ignored. Critics do not merely reflect a cultural reality — they have helped to create it. Good writing *about* food may be fueling a boom in restaurant culture.

There is a burgeoning market for candid analysis of life in the dining room, and more space than the people who run the racket admit. New voices are required to document profound changes in the way we eat — and to keep an eye on chefs, who have never been so quick to open restaurants or so anxious to abuse the customer. Later, I will look at some of the ways in which that mischief occurs. For the moment, one notes what hack and chef deny, for reasons that have little to do with valor: there has never been a better time to become a restaurant critic.

3

Accounting for Taste

The Author Admits His Past

IF YOU ASKED ME TO WHIP UP A HOLLANDAISE SAUCE, I WOULD PROBably call out for a pizza. If you wanted me to name three grapes native to Italy, I would certainly phone a friend. And if you were foolish enough to enlist my help in the preparation of some grand banquet, I would accept your invitation to dinner and later refuse to lay the table. I would do all this in good conscience, not humbled or embarrassed but determined to ensure that nobody ruins your evening.

You will learn nothing about the preparation of food in this book. There are no recipes, and I resist making judgments that hint of secret knowledge. That confession will bemuse the capable cook. Should it? Let us question the credentials of someone who dares to admit that he knows the flavor but not the facts.

In 1763, two years before the first restaurant opened, the English writer Dr. Samuel Johnson said, "You can scold a carpenter who has made you a bad table, though you cannot make a table. It is not your trade to make tables." A table with wobbly legs is no more than a poorly constructed nuisance, and the fact that one is not in the business of making tables is irrelevant. Johnson's logic is sound, and his statement exposes the idea that one needs to be an expert in a field before one dares to hold an opinion as nothing but shallow, unthinking, petit bourgeois snobbery.

Dr. Johnson once admonished a woman who had questioned his judgment on some culinary matter. Here he is, raising a finger to the dotty old turds of haute cuisine: "I, Madam, who live at a variety of good tables, am a much better judge of cookery than any person who has a very tolerable cook, but lives much at home; for his palate is gradually adapted to the taste of his cook; whereas, Madam, in trying by a wider range, I can more exquisitely judge."

This chapter, which explains how I entered the business, illustrates why anyone could now become a restaurant critic. If you dispute Johnson's logic, find my ignorance breath-defying, and cannot accept that my journey is in any way instructive, note that I have worked as a critic since the age of twenty-one. On the day I write these lines, the future is far less certain than it was back then. Part of that is due to age; the rest is unresolved.

As a child, my parents forced me to eat in most of the great French restaurants. Like many young, well-fed, middle-class couples, they dreamed of opening a place of their own, and our gastronomic Tour de France was research. So I started to judge the world's most serious cooking as my peers were learning to remove the pickles from a Big Mac.

La Colombe d'Or, in St. Paul de Vence, was a frequent destination on these culinary excursions. On becoming an adult, I was devastated to discover that this fairy-tale inn is among the most famous retreats in the south of France (it was like being introduced to an ex who is now sleeping with your kid brother). Carved into the walls of St. Paul de Vence, a medieval hilltop village, La Colombe d'Or boasts a collection of paintings by young, penniless artists, such as Chagall, Miró, and Picasso, who all donated work in exchange for food in the 1940s. There are bedrooms (unremarkable) and a heated swimming pool. The food is good, but it struggles to compete with the glamour, the art, and the view from the terrace. Diners sit at tables that are covered in crisp white linen. The atmosphere is largely dictated by the mixture of customers on any given day. Many will never come back, yet even first-timers feel as if they are always returning. One imagines such a spot; arriving confirms its existence. The customers are equally familiar. One always recognizes a face from the television, some cabaret artiste, or America's most wasted.

In La Colombe d'Or, one sits close enough to the other tables to determine the provenance of fellow diners, but not close enough to curse their cologne. Many are English, and a disproportionate number are famous resting actors, which means they're unemployed. Bitter, unguarded, and emboldened by the view, they take Nietzschean dips into darkness. Wine is consumed with determination, models are summoned and promptly ignored, rivals are loudly denounced, and the general decay of Western civilization is neatly captured in the sight of a lonely, washed-up entertainer demanding one more drink.

One takes generous gulps of the view, and in each one feels complete. The hill gives way to fields of lavender, then homes, the town of Nice, and, eventually, the Mediterranean. It shimmers in the distance, like some dream within reach or the cold wink of fate, denying one a choice in the matter.

With this invitation to reflect on life, coupled with rich, unhealthy food and a lot of buxom waitresses, La Colombe d'Or is the world's best restaurant for teenage boys. The fact that I had to share the view with anything quite so uncool as parents was, of course, a disappointment. Like most adolescents, I was loud and awkward, otherwise undistinguished. A poster pinup for the age of acne, I worshipped *Playboy,* Yeats, and the A Team, in that order. In time, I also loved the Smiths, *Being There,* and peanut-butter sandwiches. My favorite actor was Marlon Brando, the patron saint of slobs: a man who traded his looks, his career, and his mythical pulling power for an endless bowl of noodles. These details are important, because they illustrate quite how shallow and incurious my childhood was. Note the absence of long, loving odes to anything that gourmets call food.

There is only one sense in which I was a fussy eater. Unmoved by the thought that God may exist but convinced that pig would keep me out of heaven — my father is Jewish — I was wary of all comestibles, and the rituals of dining made me similarly anxious. This insecurity manifested itself in a failure even to arrive at a preferred term for the thing that diners use to erase their mistakes. I called it many things — napkin, towel, serviette, cloth, handkerchief — but thought of it principally as a small white flag for waving in the air.

Could it be said that I had a head start? After many years in boarding school, I certainly knew what bad food was, and my tour of the great French restaurants left me, quite accidentally, with an ability to identify good food. Like Dr. Johnson, I lived at a variety of tables. But was I passionate about cooking? Hardly. At the age of sixteen, the passions of a man are all too private.

My parents opened Whites on the Green in Dublin on December 8, 1985. The following week, the Irish prime minister had lunch in the restaurant three days in a row. A rogue who was loved and distrusted in equal measure, Charles Haughey thought nothing of lecturing the country on frugality while running up a million-pound overdraft and scrounging off local tycoons. That he seduced them all in the same surroundings must have given him particular pleasure.

After the politicians, there came the critics. The very first one tarnished my opinion of the trade forever. I will not forget being told, in a whisper, that the pantomime hack on table two had the power to put us out of business. He may well have been a connoisseur, and was certainly a professional alcoholic. Peter Drucker was right: we use the word *guru* because *charlatan* is too long.

That critic loved Whites, describing it as "the most hallowed address in Gourmet Ireland. . . ." He neglected to finish the sentence with the words: ". . . a land more remote and improbable than Liberal Texas." At the beginning, I used the restaurant as a tool for impressing young women, like a new tattoo or a Harley Davidson, without the obligatory ride. For about three weeks, I took full advantage of the situation and was soon imagining myself at the center of a lavish theatrical production that could only be deemed a triumph if Master White and his swell young pals were parked on table seven. When my father decided that I should stop defrauding him, he pulled a few strings and got me a job, answering the phones on a Saturday afternoon.

"Hello, Whites on the Green."

With those five words, I was introduced to adulthood in all its shamelessness. The art of getting a table is not something a child should have to witness. Bribes, excuses, try-ons, name-dropping, threats, and invocation; none of these are good for kids. After six weeks, I was assigned to an even more lowly station, under the stairs, hanging the coats. Boy, did I take coats! Charlton, Lagerfeld, Kissinger, Kennedy . . . the names do more justice to the restaurant than my recollection of the saffron risotto. I stood guard at the door to a cavernous wardrobe, just outside the ladies' bathroom. One of Britain's most prominent broadcasters fell down those stairs, after one too many bottles. I would not dream of identifying the celebrated gay novelist who was caught unscrewing the toilet-roll holder in the men's bathroom, or the opera singer who threw herself at a seventeen-year-old. Lost in the mists of time, until my career evaporates.

Out front, it was a classic silver-service job, with a mercurial French maître d' and the constant threat of some new discord. In restaurants, people arrive feeling hungry and they soon start drinking: neither state shows them at their best. Whites was the sort of place in which a politician might come to repair a marriage, loudly announcing his humility before flirting with a waitress in diplomatic French. Trained to endure such gallantry, the waitress would smile, acquiesce, and later extract the legendary tip of an affluent, horny, guilty drunk. Elsewhere, young men would demand cigars, to the fury of the poor but starstruck foodies on table nine. They chose that table because it was just within earshot of the kitchen. The chef, lately arrived from Le Gavroche, was a master of nouvelle cuisine, minimalist French nonsense that was briefly fashionable, long derided, and best followed by a bag of popcorn. Culinary masochists, the foodies longed to hear some Gallic admonition, and would pounce on a whiff of garlic, roasted, as if it settled an ancient score.

After four years of flattering strangers and frowning at waiters, my parents sold the business. Like many first-class restaurants, Whites on the Green was not vastly profitable. At that end of the market, many restaurateurs barely break even on the food. However, it is possible to make a few dollars on the wine if one buys good stuff *en primeur,* holding on to it until vintages (and prices) mature. My parents were shrewd enough to keep the building — the one sure way to make money in restaurants.

To this day, some people talk about Whites like some golden light in the distant past, while others think it is still open — a measure of public ignorance, or a compliment to the restaurant. Long closed, it has certainly opened doors for me, and I am proud of my parents. One cannot blame them for the lie that launched a career.

The fact that my family had a restaurant for four years means that I have been in a restaurant kitchen. People think I was peeling carrots in a cot. How can I presume to criticize chefs, when I don't even bother to cook? I enjoy writing and I love dining out, but a good drinker is not necessarily a good bartender. Scant knowledge of food has propelled me twice around the world, writing on humdrum subjects such as Champagne, oysters, truffles, and Sauternes. For money. Real money. I have reviewed restaurants and hotels on four continents, and I have turned an accident of birth into a career.

How I did all that:

1. Experience of the restaurant world.
2. Experience *in* the restaurant business.

Conflate these phrases. Write three reviews. You now have an excuse for badgering an editor — someone who stole your sandwiches at school or a name on the masthead. Ask him out to lunch. If he does not respond, tell his secretary that you have some very good news for him. This is all part of the procedure. Eventually, you will have lunch together. Do not, under any circumstances, drink the finger-bowl soup. Spend the first hour exchanging thoughtful pleasantries ("Have you lost weight?"). Then lower your voice.

"I want to be your restaurant critic."

"We have a restaurant critic."

"Do you?"

"Yes. Don't you read *The Globe?*"

"But of course. What's he like?"

"She's the best in the country."

Reverie. At the age of twenty-one, I phoned the editor of a local weekly and demanded a column on the spurious basis that I must know all about restaurants because everyone thinks I know all about restaurants. After several more calls, he told me to stop harassing him, which is not necessarily a bad sign. When you provoke an editor to insult you, it becomes more difficult for him to forget you. After a six-week letter-writing campaign and a couple of profoundly sycophantic phone calls, the editor agreed to pay $50 for each of my rants. This rarely covered the price of dinner, so my first reviews were effectively unpaid. They were also badly written and widely ignored, but it didn't really matter. I had a column for my precious opinions, so new and yet so dull.

Pierre Le Vicky is the man behind a chain of restaurants that threatens to destroy the notion that eating good French food is a privilege of wealth. Lunch costs £4.90 [$10]. Le Vicky is either a noble philanthropist or a lunatic. At these prices, nobody bothers to ask.

— From my first published review, of Pierre Victoire, in the
Dublin Event Guide, April 26, 1994

Get thee to Pussyville, kittens. The city's newest diner is open for business. If this place is like the Hard Rock Café in ten years, it'll be a shame. Right now it's the sort of tacky, schmaltzy hole this town sorely needs.

— From my second review, of Mr. Pussy's Café Deluxe, in the
Dublin Event Guide, May 10, 1994

Despite my windy praise, those two restaurants closed within six months. It is far easier to thrive as a restaurant critic than it is to survive as a restaurateur. In Ireland, one can quickly develop a reputation as a loudmouth, the most sincere description of all critics. It is easy to get on television, and any fool with a gripe will find an audience: flinging one's face in the public pot is no more difficult than flinging a pot in the public's face. Within three years, I had written for every major broadsheet.

Like Dr. Johnson, I care about food, for "He who does not mind his belly, will hardly mind anything else." But I took little or no interest in the kitchen, just the plate before me, and was regularly exposed as a fraud. When friends sneer at your attempt to guess the ingredients of a Welsh rarebit, it seems uncivil to pontificate on the virtue of a classical education in the culinary arts.

If things had gone according to some vague plan, the sort of plan we all pretend to have somewhere, I probably would have drifted into public relations, like many failed hacks. (Some readers may resent this characterization of the PR racket, and I am happy to apologize. As a haven for putrid scribblers, the industry is owed a great deal.) Once again, however, my parents intervened. When a notice in the *Irish Times* advertised vacancies at a new magazine called *Food and Wine,* my father implored me to apply, on the basis that the man behind it had been a customer at Whites on the Green. Short, plump, and fond of cigars, Kevin Kelly was the most successful magazine publisher in the country. Why would he want anything to do with me?

At the interview, Kelly told me that I could "possibly" have a job at *Food and Wine* if I convinced Andrew Lloyd Webber to join the new magazine as a restaurant critic. I tried and failed to seduce Lloyd Webber, but that soon proved irrelevant. The publisher had a vivid recollection of the sea bass in Whites, where the rich and famous were treated with the deference such people demand. These sundry facts did more for my career than the tens of thousands of words I had written at that point.

Starting on a salary of £11,000 ($22,000), I was sent around the country to investigate new hotels and all the same old kitchens. Ireland is an also-ran in the restaurant revolution. Unlike most European states, we have contributed little to modern cuisine, and for an island nation, we are remarkably ambivalent about fish. When smoking was banned in the country's dining rooms, it changed the price of eating out — you don't have to pay with your life — but not, alas, the quality. In public, critics rave, with good reason, about the quality of Irish produce. In private, we deride the general standard of cooking. No one says as much in print (it is like admitting defeat), and foreign journalists are kinder still. So even a reputable rag like *Condé Nast Traveler* can claim that "a new generation of local-born chefs has emerged in Ireland, and they have rediscovered and refined Irish food." This is simply not true. Most good chefs who stay in Ireland are in thrall to French cuisine, in which butter and cream sauces often feature. Butter and cream are made in Ireland. Hence the mistake: basic, lazy, all too typical. It is a mistake made by people who know nothing about food, and by those who know a great deal.★

★Reviewing the short-lived Restaurant Conrad Gallagher on Shaftesbury Avenue, the English critic Jay Rayner makes an astute observation about Gallagher's "modern Irish cooking": "This is one of those very silly phrases used simply to carve out a nonexistent niche; as far as I'm aware, seared scallops and foie gras, which is a starter here, has never been a staple dish of County Cork, or anywhere else in Ireland for that matter."

★　　★　　★

Ireland is often described as a culinary wasteland. However, the country remains a world leader in two departments: drinking you dry and quenching your thirst. Baileys is one of the world's top-selling liqueurs and Guinness is served in more countries than any other beer. At home, stout, or porter, has long been a substitute for solids, and we are now the second-largest consumers of beer on the planet. Writing in the 1950s, Flann O'Brien satirized the national thirst: "When food is scarce and your larder bare, and no rashers grease your pan, when hunger grows as your meals are rare — A pint of plain is your only man."

Our relationship with alcohol is more complicated, less romantic, than foreigners imagine. Consider the story of Tom Maher. When he died at the age of ninety-two, Maher and his wife, Mary, had spent sixty years running a men-only pub in Waterford. Despite repeated protests by feminist groups, the publican insisted that no woman was to be served at his counter. Maher closed his doors at 10 p.m. sharp each night, well before official closing time. His business ethos was simple: "I don't want to see my customer too early, too late, or too often." He never drank alcohol, although he did blend his own whiskey, which was shared with regular customers. "But only when they deserve it." After falling out with Guinness in the 1980s, Maher banned all its products from his pub. He also refused to serve smokers long before Ireland became the first country in the world to ban smoking in all bars and restaurants.

The tale of Tom Maher reveals a maverick streak in the Irish character. Amid the numb smiles of celebrity culture and the spiteful lash of commerce, distinctive voices occasionally emerge, and they deserve to be championed, just as good chefs warrant public displays of gratitude. That rarely happens with any sincerity in Dublin, where the function of a critic is to deceive: you write that everything is fine, we have an indigenous cuisine, we're getting better, there are many great restaurants, and, if you look very hard, you may well meet a leprechaun gunning down those who have the cheek to call orange juice "fresh" from a carton. When you lavish praise on just about everyone, no one is actually singled out.

In the early days, I did not dare to voice such reservations. Critics are supposed to be erudite. It was only a matter of time, I reasoned, before someone would ask me what to do with a fish knife. But I also suspected an element of foul play. Indeed, I remember taking delight in the story about that fellow who walked into the queen's bedroom, only to find her watching *Neighbours,* a soap opera. "Who's conning who?" I wondered. "Who is the real impostor? If I can talk my way into the heart of a racket, and all these people are prepared to take me seriously, what does that make them?"

There is an episode of *The Simpsons* in which Homer becomes a restaurant critic. Bart says the only way things could improve is if Homer could draw a salary for scratching his butt. Unfortunately, the demands of the job soon catch up with our hero. In the impoverished language of food criticism, most writing consists of a search for ways to avoid the word "tasty." The silent struggle in the author's mind is often more engrossing than anything he actually has to say. For "delicious," read, "I surrender." No quitter, Homer begs his daughter, Lisa, to help him write the reviews.

HOMER: So come to the Legless Frog if you want to get sick and die and leave a big garlicky corpse. PS: Parking was ample.

LISA: Dad, you're being cruel for no reason. What will people think?

HOMER: People will think what I tell them you think when you tell me what to tell them to think.

LISA: Not anymore! I don't want to be partners with a man who thinks like that!

HOMER: Nobody talks to me that way. I'm Homer Simpson, the most powerful food critic in town, who will never get his comeuppance! You hear me? *No comeuppance!*

Homer's career came to an abrupt end. In real life, however, many hacks survive for years without considering the most basic principles of criticism. In the early 1990s, I wanted to avoid that conversation. I dreaded the day on which it would be decreed that a man with a large appetite is not entitled to have an opinion about food.

When would that day come? And would I then be eaten alive?

In May 1997, a large food company invited me to join sixteen European food critics on a tour of County Sligo. I met my colleagues in a railway station at seven o'clock in the morning. Sixteen dames said, "Hello, nice to meet you," "My God, you're young," and "Beware, some of these women are poisonous." Flattered and horrified, I said nothing on the four-hour journey.

As we alighted from the train, I helped the women with their suitcases. This gesture, no more than common decency, proved wildly popular, and I was quickly adopted as a mascot, on the basis that I couldn't possibly be as vile as everyone else. Naturally, I didn't know what to say. When you enter the confidence of a food critic, you are soon engulfed in claim, counter-claim, speculation, torrid rebuke, and epic paranoia. Occupational hazards such as dipsomania, obesity, gout, dyspepsia, and food poisoning are all well documented, but the biggest killer in the business is back-stabbing. Connoisseurs hate each other with a passion that is equaled only by theater critics, who call each other things like "the frog-faced ugly sister of Mr. Toad" and "a megalomaniac who you want to see die a slow, horrible death."★

When a rookie goes out to dinner with a gang of older critics, he is not simply on his best behavior. He is expected to look and sound like an eminent gourmet; that is, like a pedigree chump who is always advertising his erudition; a person whose self-regard is complemented by good breeding, bad breath, and fetishistic reverence. It is not enough

---

★Referring, respectively, to *Time Out*'s Martin Hoyle and Ian Shuttleworth of the *Financial Times*.

to know the names of half a dozen curries or a couple of good risottos. Oh no, not anymore. Ruth Reichl, the editor of *Gourmet* magazine, says that when she started to write about food in the 1970s, critics had to know about French and Italian cooking. "Today," she writes, "you have to know about food from all over the world, and, if you don't, you have to learn about it. No credible critic today can talk about Japanese food without really having some knowledge of it."

It is true that a scholarly person such as Ruth Reichl, who was living on a commune when she decided to become a critic, may have fresh insights, and good cooks sometimes make great journalists. It is useful to know, for instance, that broccoli is better blanched than steamed, and it certainly helps to know the difference. However, there is a good deal of nonsense in this regard.

Some critics know little about cooking. More know a lot about, say, French cooking and nothing about offal, for the excellent reason that its homonym is *awful*. Most reviewers will spend time learning about *joues de boeuf* (ox cheeks) in order to stand their ground among other "experts," rather than concede their contempt for bovine entrails. This is supposed to be part of some grand play for objectivity. All it really proves is that the writer is devious and not above tokenism. Neither are particularly attractive traits.

Back in 1997, the thought of a diurnal inquisition was enough to make me queasy. I didn't want to put dinner under the microscope. I wanted to eat it. I have always liked books that are smart, short, and funny; films that engage me immediately; and conversation that is not hampered by boundary or expectation. I have neither the patience for elaborate cock-teasing nor the time to stand in line. Worse still, I am a legendary drinker. Three glasses of wine will usually leave me dizzy, and a fourth will knock me over. All these failings conspired to make me particularly vulnerable on the night of May 16.

After three days of nodding assent and too much free claret (the proper position on people who dine out for a living: hate them or become one), I was weary. They say that red wine is good for you; hacks say it more than most. I now knew why. At dinner that night with all those reviewers, I began to wonder if the vitriol that passed for conversation was healthy. When one critic, Lady F, asked after a rival's husband — a notorious philanderer — the victim struck back by muttering something pithy about sex and the twentieth century. A third critic entered the fray, in what seemed like a bid to keep the peace, by asking no one in particular the following question: "What do you think of the soup?"

There was silence at the table, which was warning enough. When formidable women hold their tongue as one, no man should lose the run of his. Try slurring the following:

> "Beg pardon, ladies . . . I will now take the liberty, yes, the liberty, of answering that question by attempting to describe the soup." [Pause.] "It is hot, full of flavor and a bit too rich, and . . . I don't know how to make that soup. I wouldn't know how to make it . . . In fact, I don't think I have ever made a bowl of soup. Ever. You see, ladies, I don't really know how to cook." [Long pause.] "Does that surprise you?"

Silence, briefly. Before I had time to do further damage, a voice at the other end of the table muttered, "Sweetie, relax. You're in much better company than you think."

Half the critics met this remark with a sharp intake of breath. The other half chuckled, as you might chuckle at some piece of good news. I too smiled — a bashful grin, and premature. More silence. How did I make such a fool of myself? Would I ever have dinner in Dublin again? Unlikely. *Dammit,* impossible — would sooner read a recipe than meet another critic.

As I began to contemplate the respective virtues of razor blade and rope, the great Lady F dug into her soup, raised the spoon to her mouth, imbibed, and loudly retched.

"Jesus!" she cried. "Did someone say soup? Damn thing tastes like gravy!"

The indomitable bitch had a heart after all. It was the kindest thing I had heard in three days, and it changed the tone of dinner. The following morning, I helped to carry the suitcases once again and reflected on the trip, which had proved instructive. In seventy-two hours, I had acquired some allies, a delicate head, and a little understanding. In a hotel bed, alone, when all they can hear is the distant flushing of a loo, critics know that what they do is more of a scam than a proper occupation. If humans earned prizes for ingenuity, getting paid to consume good food and wine would merit some special award. Cooks who moonlight as critics cannot quite believe their luck, and the rest of us think the dream will end in the morning. No wonder we're all so insecure.

But enough of hesitation.

Returning to Dublin, I resolved to put the whole thing behind me. It belonged in the past, and it did not serve a purpose. Doubt? How dare I indulge in something so awkward, when so many frauds ran restaurants? Where was the profit in addressing misgivings about my own profession? Profession? Ha! That word could at last be used with impunity.

All hail the sultan of soup, cocky little bastard on the make.

"He thinks I'm a good cook in the same way I think he's good in bed."

4

Kitchen Con

How the Racket Works

IN 1963, THE BISHOP OF KERRY TOLD THE ACTRESS DIANA DORS TO leave the town of Tralee. The bishop was disgusted by whispers of a cabaret performance that left nothing to the imagination. Chased by reporters and a clutch of aging bachelors, the actress decamped to Dublin, where she took a suite in the city's best hotel. Every night at six o'clock, two bodyguards collected a tray from the hotel kitchen. On it stood a pot of tea and a freshly baked apple tart, both for the resident celebrity. Each night, the kitchen porters made vulgar remarks about sex, tarts, and Diana Dors. On the fourth and final night of her stay, a chef took the freshly baked tart, removed the lid, and spread a thin layer of bodily fluids over puréed apple. Then he smiled at his colleagues, replaced the lid of the tart, and garnished it with a sprig of mint. No one intervened. The plate was later returned to the kitchen, without so much as a crumb of complaint.

Kitchen Confidential is full of similar stories. Anthony Bourdain's best-selling memoir about his early days as a chef in New York is a homage to the "whacked-out moral degenerates, dope fiends, refugees . . . drunks, sneaks, thieves, sluts and psychopaths" who work the pass each night. Are critics any less criminal? Look at the title of this book. Call it an act of worship if you wish. It was in fact a steal. Such acts are typical in the restaurant world, which is full of rip-off artists. Imitation explains why so many second-rate chefs survive. But a cook who dares to tell the truth? Now that's unusual. No wonder he did so well.

Given the behavior of those who were privy to the apple-tart incident, it may surprise you to learn that men who cook for a living are quite a delicate bunch. Indeed, with the possible exception of gay hoteliers, there is no more sensitive group of people than chefs. Scientists have recently discovered that they take more offense than Mary Whitehouse. That's why I am always shocked when they threaten to sue, or, worse still, punch my lights out. Both of these activities require a certain steeliness.

Some chefs even go to court over good reviews. In August 2004, one Phil Romano filed a sixteen-page lawsuit over a review of his new restaurant in the *Dallas Morning News*. Romano was furious with critic Dotty Griffith after she dared to give the restaurant Il Mulino New York — another homage, no doubt — eleven and a half stars out of a possible fifteen. Griffith had claimed that Il Mulino's vodka sauce was "finished with butter," and that the "delicious" porcini ravioli "whispered of Gorgonzola."

"I don't have any Gorgonzola in the whole kitchen," fumed Romano, "and there's no butter in that vodka sauce."

The newspaper issued a statement. Note the hasty, withering timbre. Sounds like a middle-aged lawyer who was stuck in the office on a Friday night, wife on the phone, dinner getting cold:

> It's clear from the complaint that the plaintiff recognizes that the review was an expression of opinion, protected by the First Amendment. If this sort of claim were allowed to proceed, newspapers, magazines, and others would have to defend unfavorable reviews of restaurants, books, movies, and the like constantly. Since claims like this are not allowed under the law, the plaintiff has tried to concoct claims other than defamation — but those

efforts cannot hide the fact that they simply disagree with the review. The disagreement, fortunately, is not grounds for a lawsuit.

Romano was undaunted. "They hide behind opinion and free speech, which is fine," he told a reporter. "I'm trying to critique the critiquer."

The case was dropped, or settled, quickly. Life went on. Romano is still in business. He says it remains robust. Good for him? Not really. For the last ten years, I have been issued with lurid threats on a weekly basis. Some of them are quite serious. No one likes to spend much time in court, as lawyers are so crooked that they even make chefs look honest. Fortunately, I can laugh off most complaints. The rest are *sub judice*.

There are several examples of culinary revenge that do not involve lawyers, which thus deserve to be celebrated. I am thinking of staff at a restaurant, Villager, where:

> . . . the rosti was so thick and chewy it bore a strong resemblance to gardening twine, my partner could hardly touch the frazzled remains of some poor beast . . . and the best part of the evening was when we were told that we couldn't order dessert, because the kitchen was closed — at 9:30 p.m.

The man who penned these remarks, Richard Bath, is a sports editor and occasional restaurant critic at a Scottish newspaper. He clearly thought Villager was fair game: "Not since I left the Lighthouse in Leith with my stomach churning, my ears bleeding and my wallet empty have I vowed never to return to a restaurant. But vow I did."

The restaurant's response was equally unambiguous. A large sign appeared on the wall of the dining room: "RICHARD BATH WEARS LADIES' UNDERWEAR."

The most famous Irish chef is a young man called Conrad Gallagher. When a colleague of mine, Helen Lucy Burke, had the pleasure of dining at his flagship restaurant, Peacock Alley, Gallagher decided to spare her the nuisance of writing it up by issuing a lawyer's letter in which it was alleged that on the night in question:

> Helen Lucy Burke . . . appeared to be intoxicated, made very
> little sense to talk to, in addition to slurring her words, and also
> made unnecessary disparaging remarks to Mr. Gallagher's staff,
> e.g., "Can you wrap this up, I want to feed it to my blind pussy?"

Wine often clouds a critic's judgment. There are questions to be asked
of all hacks in this regard. Answers, if any, are slurred. However, Helen Lucy Burke is a woman of rare integrity. Her moral probity is even
celebrated in a song by Christy Moore, who refers to her "mattress-
sniffing" days as a hotel critic. Gallagher's decision to issue a solicitor's
letter was designed to deflect attention from the contents of the review
itself. Rather than issuing a strenuous denial, Burke's editor, John
Ryan (he now publishes a magazine called *New York Dog*) decided to
publish the solicitor's letter alongside the review — which, by the way,
was quite sympathetic — allowing readers to decide who stumbled on
the job: who had a leg to stand on, and who was utterly legless. The
article was headlined "The Peacock, the Critic and the Blind Pussy."
It was an ingenious move, and marked, I think, the beginning of the
end for Gallagher's empire.

In 2004, one Sarah Roe was accosted by the chef Tom Aikens as
she tried to leave his London restaurant. "Where," asked Aikens, "is
my teaspoon?" The businesswoman had just settled a bill of £536
($1,072), but Aikens wouldn't let her go until the spoon was found —
on another table. What does this anecdote tell us about chefs? Does it
illustrate their attention to detail? Does it suggest that too much time
in the kitchen can also cloud a man's judgment? Perhaps it means that
Aikens was wrong this time, but right, in general, to prance around
like a young Inspector Clouseau.

I am suspicious of chefs who try to adopt the moral high ground,
because the restaurant business is, and always has been, a front for
the Kitchen Con. There is no spite in that remark — critics are just
as greedy. Great chefs are entitled to have delusions, and figures like
Gallagher and Aikens deserve support. At least they know how to
cook. It's crooks with a rusty knife — and all their unscrupulous

bosses — who epitomize the Kitchen Con. It is they who deserve to be exposed. Here, then, are twenty ways in which restaurants abuse their customers. I sincerely hope that you aren't familiar with every single one.

That Special Feeling

In a perfect world, specials would be, well, special. Made from seasonal produce that doesn't last long enough to become part of an à la carte menu, they would principally appeal to regular customers who want a little variety — and particularly good value. In the real world, specials are an excuse for restaurants to extract maximum profit from stale food. That Special Feeling is being ripped off.

Two-Sittings Tyranny

They used to call it the hospitality business. Hospitality means "kindness in welcoming strangers or guests." Have you ever told anyone that unless they turn up for dinner in your house at half past seven and leave by five to nine, they're going to be turned away? That is what a hostess is employed to do. The tyranny of two sittings is a recent invention. It's one of the few good reasons for welcoming the prospect of a nice long recession.

When Bread Means Dough

The cost of bread is traditionally factored into menu prices, just like electricity, say, or the rent on the owner's mistress's apartment. Lately, however, restaurateurs have grown tired of "giving things away for free." Naturally, the price of your bread does not become apparent until you have received the check.

The Big Ticket

An odious creature called "the menu engineer" — a New York original — has discovered that expensive dishes are, psychologically, a profitable move. It doesn't matter if no one orders the $47 filet mignon, as it makes the $34 salmon look cheap. Putting one obscenely pricey dish on your menu will make the average price of a meal go up, even if no one orders the most expensive dish.

Price, Quality, Bollocks

For every mid-priced restaurant that deserves to die a quick, painful death, there are at least two expensive ones that deserve the same fate. Price does not always equal quality, but try telling that to the mugs of the world. If it's expensive, they think, it must be good. Not necessarily. Good restaurant criticism can save you money. It takes courage to learn this lesson.

The White Hole

How many times have you ended up paying nearly 30 percent of your check as a tip? Many restaurants slap on a "discretionary" 12.5 percent service charge, without even bothering to ask you if everything was all right. Then they hand you a credit-card slip with a hole in the space marked "service." Being a civilized but slightly tipsy human being, you assume that service has not been added. And you put it on again.

The Hot New Place

Journalists are paid to promote restaurants that would otherwise flop. The payment either takes the form of a benefit in kind ("Why don't you and your pals come for dinner and drinks on Friday?") or old-fashioned cash. Nobody likes to talk about this, because it doesn't make anyone look good — except, of course, that exciting new place for dinner on Fridays.

Celebrity Endorsements

A variation on The Hot New Place. Take one frightful new restaurant, find a couple of B-list celebrities, convince a journalist to review it, and bingo! Suddenly it's The Hottest New Place In Town. For evidence of this phenomenon, read the social diary in any mid-market tabloid for longer than two weeks. In time, you will see what I mean.

The Menu as Thesis

It's dinner you're after, not the new Dylan Thomas. Flowery descriptions that are hard to understand can usually be translated thus: "Watch us rip you off." Contrary to culinary wisdom, reading a menu should not require a Ph.D. The only time it does is when the chef thinks himself a poet as well as an artist, in the fashion of Adolf Hitler.

Side-Order Madness

Customers in a French place down the road are invited to pay $43.95 for eight shrimp — with a wedge of lemon and a sprig of chervil. Would not feed a child of seven. The waiter, trained in the art of up-selling, says some accompaniment may be necessary. After paying $8 each for potatoes and vegetable of the day, the dish now costs $51.95 *plus* service. That's haute cuisine prices in a mid-market brasserie. Happens all over the world.

The Dining Room as Brothel

Chefs who moan about the power of critics are usually the first to send them out another appetizer, extra truffle shavings, free dessert, petits fours . . . anything that might corrupt a jaded hack. Such largesse makes whores of everyone, but often does the job. "Chefs who send out free dishes are like divorcées in fishnet tights," says a colleague. "You know there's something going on, but you're happy to be taken for a ride."

Organic Food

If flying from London to New York is morally indefensible, as many environmentalists claim, so is ordering an organic, free-range chicken that has traveled thousands of miles from farm to plate. And organic farmers send fruit to the other side of the world all the time. If you insist on moral equivalence, don't be surprised when it bites you in the ass. Ordering organic food is a good idea. *Local* organic is better still.

"Service" Charge

The greatest myth of all time — and one that I will return to later. For the moment, a simple question: Wouldn't it be nice if restaurant owners decided to pay their staff? After all, the only other people who depend on tips to feed their kids are lap dancers. What does that tell you about the status of waiters in the restaurant world?

The Wine List

Designed to intimidate, this leather-bound book of lies is the most amusing thing in most restaurants. Sit back, relax, and marvel at the audacity of comparing the aroma of grape juice to that of beets. Stand up and shout: "At last! A wine that smells like boiled beets!" Laugh at the cost of famous French plonk. It's often wiser to stick to the house wines, as the markups on everything else are so high.

What Is the Difference Between a Jeroboam and a Rehoboam?

According to James Joyce, the most beautiful word in the English language is "cuspidor," which is a synonym for "spittoon." No one knew more about words than Joyce. His counterpart in the booze racket is Robert Mondavi, who developed a taste for wine at the age of three, after discovering that Chardonnay improves the taste of cornflakes. "All of a sudden you enjoy your breakfast much more." Today, the grand old man of Napa Valley is older and less feisty, but his dedication to the grape has not diminished; indeed, Robert Mondavi is one of the few people who can call wine "a way of life" without inviting snickers.

In his autobiography, Mondavi misidentified the five first growths of Bordeaux, by substituting Pétrus for Latour. This is a grave error, as serious in its way as the day Joan Rivers forgot to do her makeup. When you discover that a figure of Mondavi's stature can make such an elementary mistake, you realize that, sooner or later, wine is going to get you. You can respond in two ways: by studying oenology for several decades or making a virtue of your ignorance.

If, like me, you have the inclination to drink wine but not the erudition, do not be scared of a sommelier. Rather, throw your arms to heaven and implore him to get you something cheap and cheerful. If that doesn't provoke a response (this is the moment when French sommeliers forget all their English), tell him you want something fruity, firm, with just a hint of bull. This has the double benefit of disarming him and exonerating you.

It is time to dispel the myth that people who love dining out must know a lot about wine. What is the difference between a jeroboam and a rehoboam? There is only one sensible answer to this question: Who cares?

The Devil Inside

Waiter and customer have a lot in common. Each lingers under the delusion that lunch is on the way, neither has more than a passing interest in the other, and both are at the mercy of an ill-tempered thug in a dirty white hat.

Malicious Drinking Games

In many restaurants, the majority of profits are made on what you drink, not what you eat. Fay Maschler, the doyenne of British critics, cites some of the pathetically obvious ruses that restaurateurs employ to inflate your bill:

> Warm encouragement to have a drink in the bar before going to the table, pouring more wine and water after every sip, bringing petits fours that you might not want so that coffee can be charged as if it is a separate course.

Mutton Dressed as Lamb

A portion of farmed salmon costs one dollar. It can be sold for $28. Alchemy? Fraud. "In order to perform this miracle," says one insider, "you have to indulge in a little window dressing: sprigs of watercress at tuppence each; fancy, French-sounding waiters; a Provençal menu borrowed from Elizabeth David." Don't forget the Chilean sea bass that is actually Patagonian toothfish, the wasabi that is actually dyed horseradish, or the truffled potatoes that are made with supermarket mushrooms and a little truffle oil.

Fresh-Faced Liars

Orange juice: available even in tropical dictatorships. On this subject, concentrate is the enemy of good taste. So, too, are cartons or containers of any sort. The distance between "fresh" orange juice and orange juice that is squeezed to order is roughly the height of the liar who sold you the former. Bring him down to size, which does require squeezing to a pulp.

French Fiction Food

Presenting an English-speaking diner with a menu in French is the very antithesis of hospitality. It is like asking a neighbor around for tea, then loudly noting that she didn't even bother to bring you flowers. Worse still is the use of fraudulent foreign words to describe dishes inaccurately. Toast is not bruschetta, and a cappuccino of white beans has nothing to do with coffee. Chefs: change "stew" to "daube" and double the price!

The Well-Reviewed Kip

Throughout this book, you will find reasons for doubting the word of self-styled experts who would have you believe they are somehow qualified to tell you if a restaurant is any good. The ordinary diner is often in a better position to review a restaurant, as many critics are instantly identified and treated with special care.

5

The Truth about Guidebooks

The Author Loses a Job

With jaw-dropping pomposity, the *Good Hotel Guide* reports that, in the past year, it hasn't received a single report from a member of the public about Sharrow Bay, so has dropped it. How self-important, how utterly, contemptuously vain do you have to be before you take notice of the people who *don't* write you letters?

— A. A. Gill

I OFTEN GET URGENT PHONE CALLS FROM EDITORS IN LONDON WHO have each devised the brilliant idea of running an article about the New Gael Force or some such twaddle. I am also asked to write loving profiles of Ireland's best chefs, as if that task does not require the skills of a novelist. Most of the time, I decline these invitations, but sometimes the money is just too good.

In 2004, I was asked to contribute to the *Dorling Kindersley Eyewitness Guide to Ireland*. I liked the guidebooks in that series — distinctive, polished, and Cultural with a capital C. Together with their sister imprint, the Rough Guides — both are published by Penguin — they have always seemed well-researched and independent. (Until quite recently, I had a sympathetic view of all guides. They are, I thought, a form of insurance. If you're going to spend a fortune on a vacation or a big night out, an expert opinion is valuable, and rarely expensive in the context of the larger investment.) The lady with the clipped vowels mentioned a reasonable fee, and the deadline was mercifully close, which meant I would soon get paid. Alas, I was far too busy, trying to save a business. So I suggested the name of a friend — let's call her Arabella — who was trying to break into journalism.

"Very reliable girl," I assured the editor, "and polite. Very polite."

This is code language for: "She's Irish, that's true, but she isn't in the IRA."

Arabella got the job on the back of my seven-word reference. It sounded like a dream assignment: to write up a short report on sixty hotels, some of them gems in remote and beautiful places. Three weeks later, she rang up, fuming.

"Trevor, you said this was journalism."

"It is . . . Isn't it?"

"No. It's research."

"Often the way. They're obviously determined to get it right."

"What?"

"Travel? You must be doing a lot of travel?"

"I haven't left the house."

Arabella's job was to be one of a team of contributors revealing where travelers should stay in Ireland by whatever means necessary — except that her particular contribution did not involve her actually going to stay in the hotels.

"I'm sorry, I really am. I thought it was a plush assignment."

"Well, that's the English for you," she said.

"You know," I replied, "the funny thing is, I actually blame the French."

"What? The French have nothing to do with it."

"Oh no, I assure you, the English have nothing on the French."

The English are minor transgressors. The French are to blame for everything. To understand what that means, and why it is pertinent in the context of guidebooks, you have to go back over 200 years, to the dawn of public gastronomy. You have to return to Paris.

The restaurant business has always been plagued by a lack of hospitality. Even at the moment of conception, critics lined up to damn the poor fellow who dared to feed all comers. Boulanger was a tavern keeper. One evening, in the spring of 1765, he decided to serve a dish of sheep's feet simmered in a white sauce, as a restorative, or *restorante*. Until then, taverns and cafés had served alcohol and coffee. Nobody was quite obtuse enough to think that there might be more money in food. "Come unto me," scrawled Boulanger on his door, "all ye that labor in the stomach, and I will restore you." For his troubles, he was taken to court by the guild of *traiteurs,* for infringing on their monopoly on the sale of cooked foods. After a lot of publicity, much fanning of feathers, and a frank exchange of views in parliament, Boulanger was allowed to continue.

"I went to dine at the restaurateur's place," wrote Denis Diderot. "One is treated well there but has to pay dearly for it." This gripe, or some version thereof, has been fashionable ever since. It is the first and last word in restaurant criticism.

In 1789, Marie Antoinette made an ill-advised remark about cake (later echoed by Margaret Thatcher, in every single act of her political career). After the French Revolution, cooks left the service of aristocrats, guilds — and their privileges — were abolished, and the chop-house business suddenly took off. There were fewer than a hundred restaurants in Paris in 1789. There were 500 in 1804.

The world's first restaurant guide — the *Almanach des Gourmands* — was launched in 1803, and with it a new religion, *le monde Gourmand.* Broadly composed of people who want to eat out tonight, this secular faith has two core beliefs: "I don't want to cook" and "I don't have to cook." Gourmands are always mumbling about some new restaurant on the other side of town, and they read reviews with the same fervor that a pastor brings to scripture.

The man behind the guide was a misogynist who wrote with mechanical hands. Alexandre-Balthazar-Laurent Grimod de la Reynière was the sort of friend who gets you to pay for lunch, then asks for the receipt. The *Almanach des Gourmands* was a best-seller, and Grimod was the first journalist to taste real power in victuals. Inevitably, the jury system that he set up to assess restaurants was accused of corruption, but the public didn't seem to mind. His guide was reprinted eight times between 1803 and 1813.

Ten years later, Jean Anthelme Brillat-Savarin published a book of philosophical musings on food. *The Physiology of Taste* was the grandfather of all those heavy books on light-hearted subjects. Brillat-Savarin started his career as a lawyer, became a politician, was banished during the Reign of Terror, and spent three years as a refugee in America, where he labored as both a violinist and a language teacher. Then he returned to France, where he eventually became a member of the Supreme Court of Appeal. He liked nothing better than the company of friends in a very good restaurant, where he said some remarkably asinine things: "People predestined to Gourmandism are in general of medium height; they have round or square faces, bright eyes, small foreheads, short noses, full lips, and rounded chins."

Brillat-Savarin's favorite restaurant was owned by Beauvilliers, the author of the classic *L'Art du Cuisinier*. Today, it seems vaguely comical that one of the first great restaurants in Paris was called La Grande Taverne de Londres. One assumes that the chef was pitching for tourist business, and not expressing admiration. Either way, it didn't work. Like so many chefs who have followed in his wake, Beauvilliers went bust trying to prove that restaurants aren't a rich man's game.

"Beauvilliers had a prodigious memory," wrote Brillat-Savarin. "He recognized and welcomed people whom he had not seen for twenty years, people who may only have eaten at his restaurant once or twice. He would advise which dish not to take, which to snap up, and would then order a third one, which no one else would have thought of . . . but this role of a host lasted but a moment, and, having accomplished it, he would vanish. A little while later, the amount of the dinner bill and the bitterness of paying it showed clearly that one had dined with a great restaurateur."

The culinary arts have long benefited from innovation in other quarters. Electricity revolutionized cooking in the home, pots and pans were improved by NASA, and the development of microwave technology has enabled millions of take-home plebs such as myself to run the risk of serious contamination. Thus it almost seems appropriate that the oldest and most forbidding force in restaurant criticism is a branch of the motor industry.

In 1900, the Michelin tire company published a free guide to hotels, restaurants, and garages in France. They introduced the famous star-rating system in 1926. Today, there are twenty-six restaurants with three stars in France. They are not so much restaurants as places of pilgrimage, where the faithful rich worship at the altar of good taste. There is something tacky about all this, but nobody wants to go into it. Like boutique Californian wines, Michelin three-star restaurants are inviolable. There is an artist at work, and one is not encouraged to wonder how many mouths the cost of a single meal could feed.

Michelin inspectors claim to make anonymous visits to over forty thousand restaurants in ten countries. Are there many inspectors? In Britain, approximately ten. Restaurants, oil, and global defense are the only industries in which millions of people and billions of dollars are so dependent on such a small, esoteric clique.

Sometimes, inspectors will return to the same restaurant several times. Waitresses are told to look out for middle-aged men who come alone, eat too much, and book in names that expose a secret longing. They use monikers like Sinatra (Jacques) or Monroe (Michel) and according to Michelin they must have "an appreciation for the finer things in life, such as architecture, art, and antiques." What they really care about, however, is "what's on the plate," as the new director of the organization put it in his first interview in 2005. A Michelin inspector would describe a meal in a Munich beer hall in the fall of 1939 without reference to war or the blank look of fear in the Jewish waiter's eyes. He would, however, find space to reflect on the texture of the bratwurst.

Brillat-Savarin described a top gastronomic experience as "good food cooked simply and eaten in surroundings in which everyone can feel at home." Where does that leave Michelin? A critic is not someone who is paid to keep peasants off the land. We are supposed to open the gates to all, not hide behind some culinary dogma. If we promote the myth that good cooking is some esoteric French art that you fools will never understand, or, indeed, that dining rooms should feel like somber, self-important shrines, we are failing to serve the public. For too long, that's what has happened at Michelin.

In an era when so much cooking is homogenous or just plain bad, a Michelin plaudit still carries weight. At the top level, however, the guide is increasingly marginal. François Simon of *Le Figaro* is one of the most respected critics in France. "When the new edition came out this week," he said in March 2005, "it felt as if we were greeting an old aunt who is hopelessly outdated yet gives her opinion on everything. You love her because she is part of the family. You will always love her, but my goodness, when the Red Guide opens its mouth, you look at a corner of the ceiling."

There are alternatives to the nosy aunt. The best of them are *Le Pudlo Paris* and *Le Pudlo France*. Both guides are edited by Gilles Pudlowski, a talkative, twice-divorced, middle-aged hero of anyone who finds it hard not to scoff at Michelin. Pudlowski thinks nothing of accepting free meals and describes anonymity as "an idiotic idea." "Restaurateurs know a critic when they see one," he told a newspaper last year. "What counts is honesty, whether they know you or not. Being incognito guarantees neither the reviewer's competence nor his judgement."

Gilles Pudlowski spent five years working for Henri Gault and Christian Millau, the men who created the *GaultMillau* guide. It uses a comprehensive twenty-point and four-toque system, which suits the educated Frenchman: in the baccalaureate, everything is marked out of twenty. Although their guidebook is less vaunted nowadays, when they first started working together in the late 1960s, Millau and Gault grabbed Paris by the stomach and famously "gave Michelin heartburn."

That is quite an honor. It now falls to Jamie Oliver, whose show, *Le Chef Nu,* had more viewers than any cooking program in the history of France. To the disgust of old-school gourmets, several million people tuned in "to see," as one critic put it, "what the impertinent rogue is trying to cook this week." With his defiantly populist agenda and food-is-fun mantra, Oliver dared to play the French at their own game. "However much one snickers," commented *Le Parisien,* "the country of jelly has given birth to the new star of world gastronomy."

The thirty-one-year-old Essex Boy is one of the few Englishmen to have influenced French cuisine. He couldn't have done it at a more delicate moment. In 2003, a chef, Bernard Loiseau, committed suicide after he was downgraded in the *GaultMillau* guide. All over France, foodies debate a rash of culinary scandals with the same intensity that Americans reserve for discussing the sex life of Paris Hilton. From the war against McDonald's to widespread allegations of corruption among critics, the French, who haven't won a war for 200 years, are putting themselves in the dock once more.

In the spring of 2005, the debate turned rancorous when a former inspector made a series of allegations after Michelin fired him for violating a confidentiality clause in his contract. Pascal Rémy's account of sixteen years and 10,000 meals with Michelin exposed one of the most secretive corporations in France, accusing it of favoritism, of cutting corners, and of duping readers:

> "More than a third of the twenty-seven French three-star restaurants keep that status because they are considered untouchable."
>
> "The guide is manipulated by aggressive letter-writing campaigns that can make or sabotage a restaurant."
>
> "There are only five full-time inspectors in France, each testing about two hundred restaurants a year, so the time between visits for the nearly four thousand restaurants can be well over two years. It's a myth that restaurants are inspected every year."
>
> "It is no longer a priority to look for the good small places in the heart of France. The goal is to bring in money. We have to go to the important places, the big-name restaurants, the big groups — that's what they say at Michelin now."
>
> "To save time and increase efficiency, Michelin staff look through other guides to see whether these have stumbled upon a young and talented chef."

Michelin rejects those charges. On the day that Rémy's book was published, the company took out full-page advertisements in national newspapers, lamenting the attack on its integrity. "France is the laughing stock of the world, faced with the unrelenting efforts of some to destroy its symbols." This is a touching defence of the little red book, and one can understand why the company is keen to protect a guide that sells 500,000 copies a year — 10 times more than its nearest rival. But sometimes Michelin has only itself to blame. In February 2005, 50,000 copies of its Belgian edition had to be pulped, after high marks were awarded to a restaurant that was "inspected" when it was still a building site.

Marco Pierre White once claimed that critics attack the guide because they are jealous about not inspiring the same respect from chefs. Wrong, replied Jonathan Meades in *The Times*. "It gets attacked precisely because it is respected by chefs and no one else. It offers chefs an annual assessment, triumphs and private griefs which cannot concern the outside world. It causes restauration to become inward-looking and to concentrate on pleasing Michelin inspectors rather than the run of customers."

The debate has now moved on: many chefs are weary of critical acclaim and are much more concerned with putting bums on seats. When Alain Senderens of Lucas Carton decided to close his three-star restaurant in Paris and reopen it as a simple brasserie, he admitted that he had grown tired of the "senseless race" for restaurant ratings and the "indecent" sums charged for the privilege of sampling haute cuisine. "I want to do something different," he said, "that will be three star in my heart."

Rosettes do not pay the rent. When Matthias Dahlinger asked Michelin to take back his one-star rating in 2003, he explained, "Just to be eligible, you have to have a minimum of 250 wines on your menu, not to mention scores of aperitifs and a host of other items designed to cater to the most discriminating palate."

It is not just the cost of opening some culinary temple that deters many younger chefs, nor the difficulty of acquiring a prized third star. They have realized that there is more money to be made from simpler dining. In France, a thirty-five-hour week and high taxes and social-security charges make it particularly hard to survive at the top. "The law encourages fraud," said Sir Terence Conran recently, "because it's so hard to survive if you're honest." Another Englishman, Robert Saunders, opened a restaurant in Cannes. Lauded by Michelin, it was forced to close after three years. Saunders agrees that there is "an immense temptation" to avoid taxes by paying staff in cash.

So there is the potential for systematic corruption in the French restaurant business, and the state implicitly endorses it, by making it so hard to survive without being fraudulent. As if to address the situation, the French government has created an Institute for Higher Studies in Taste, Gastronomy, and Table Arts. Will living in the past serve France tomorrow? The aim is noble enough. There is, after all, much to recommend classical French cuisine. But the initiative may be too late. "I know it is hard for the French to hear," said Alain Ducasse recently, "but one can eat as well in New York or Milan as in Paris."

Most French people would rather choke on a Big Mac than admit the right of, say, America to claim some culinary greatness. In the meantime, a cheeky young pup is teaching the French to cook under their very noses. With no little glee, *The Economist* recently noted that many brasseries in Paris "have sunk into mediocrity, serving up wilting lettuce leaves and dehydrated *confit de canard,* and rejecting foreign influences. In the home of gastronomy, why try anything new? Leave that, it seems, to the lad from the land of lamb with mint-jelly."

Ouch.

I explained all this to Arabella. I don't think she listened to a word — not even the diversion I made to reflect on the French taxation system. She was furious. And it was all my fault.

"OK," I said. "I know how you feel. I really do."

"It's ridiculous," she replied. "How can I recommend something without trying it out? It's not fair to the owner or the readers, and it makes a fool of me. I don't like it one bit."

"Listen, at least they don't have to pay to get into the guide. I mean, look at Alastair Sawday."

"Oh, come on," she snapped. "They won't foot the bill for staying in these places. I've been to maybe twenty. I mean, I can just about remember what ten of them are like. Fine. For the other forty, I've got two choices. I ring up the owners and faithfully type what terrible comments they make about themselves — or I paraphrase the reviews from other guidebooks."

"Right . . ."

"So don't talk to me about Alastair *bloody* Sawday!"

"OK," I cried, "this is good! Now you know how I feel. But you know what? It's worse than you think. Far worse!"

Idle provocation. It didn't work. She said nothing, just sat there, sulking. Forever. I had no option. I had to do something to justify the claim. You see, I also have a guidebook story. It doesn't reflect too well on me, but just then, I suppose, dignity wasn't the point. I was trying to save a friendship.

At a dinner party in 1979, Tim and Nina Zagat asked their guests to name their favorite restaurants. "After the tenth glass of wine," recalls Tim Zagat, "a friend of ours . . . became very publicly critical of the restaurant critic of the *New York Times*. He was not particularly sober and criticized this person with histrionic force. After listening to him for some time, I said, 'Each of you write down a list of ten friends.' We started with 200 people. The idea is that a large group of people has a statistically greater chance of coming up with an accurate assessment than a single person."

Twenty-five years later, the Zagats own the world's best-selling restaurant guides. The husband-and-wife team work with 250,000 surveyors, whose sole reward for reviewing meals is a copy of the guide. Each crimson-red book is the product of reader recommendations, and the reviews take the form of a stew in which "hit and miss" slurs sit beside "rave" endorsements, in between bits of "wacky" humor.

A 2002 report in *Business Week* revealed that thousands of surveys are sent into Zagat each day:

> The seven-person research team is kept busy all year tabulating the results into numerical ratings, city by city. From there, the data are sent to [the] 20-person editorial staff, to be distilled into pithy

reviews. "It's all about the idea of listening to other people, a consumer democracy," says Tim.

And who are these mysterious people-critics? Have they trained for years? Do they all know how to prepare a banquet? "[Our contributors] could be food and wine society members," says Zagat, "or men and women who eat out as a way of life, like executives."★

In other words, the Zagat guides are allegedly written by people like you. Their popularity (700,000 copies of the New York guide are bought every year) suggests that diners have more influence than critics. Ostensibly, this is cause for celebration, as dedicated amateurs are often more astute than self-styled experts. You keep good restaurants alive when critics have abandoned a chef, and you also provide more publicity. Eighty-three percent of restaurant business comes from word-of-mouth referrals. Tim Zagat calls it consumer democracy. Others say gossip.

Picture the scene: a newly opened bistro in the West Village, called Rare Asian Food for Rich Occidentals.

"You know, this grass-bread stuff is unique to Tibet."

"Yes, but it's ghastly, isn't it?"

"Ghastly. But *unique.*"

"I prefer that lovely Korean place we went to last week. Wonderful decor. It's not far from here. Have you been?"

★"That's a load of hornswoggling humbug," writes Charlie Suisman on the Manhattan User's Guide Web site. "Zagat doesn't select surveyors — anyone can play. While it's true that they could be wine society members or executives, it's equally true that they could not be. And since when do executives have the edge on judging food? Besides, that's an awfully elitist notion for a supposedly democratic guide."

"No, should we?"

"Yes, of course, but only for the dumplings. They're quite extraordinary, like a little taste of Paris in the amniotic sac of South East Asia. And the waiter was divine."

"We had the most amazing lunch yesterday with Mike and Suzanne at this new Italian around the corner.

"The most amazing. *Ever.* And we've been to Cipriani — in *Rome!*"

There is no Cipriani in Rome, which is where the damn critics come back into the picture. In 2003, I was asked to contribute to the *Zagat European Cities Survey.* One of seventy guidebooks published by the company each year, it remains unknown to most Irish people — one of several reasons why I hesitated when offered the assignment.

The Zagat credo sounds immensely reasonable: "Rating a restaurant on the basis of hundreds or even thousands of experiences [is] inherently more fair and accurate than relying on one reviewer and just a few meals." However, the company has its own critics. Is Zagat a competition to find the best restaurant, they ask, or a beauty pageant?

Zagat is democratic in the sense that it is open to abuse. Respondents could, in theory, evaluate meals that were eaten ten years ago or meals they *never* had. Established places score highly, as diners are more inclined to recommend restaurants they already eat in frequently. Anyone can manipulate the results by mounting a campaign to flatter or deride. "Handsome," "gregarious" restaurateurs can abuse the system. But perhaps most importantly, the ultimate power lies not with the consumer but with the editor. He or she is responsible for choosing comments that represent the "average" customer experience, and even when the comments don't tally with the editor's opinion, one can simply ignore the findings. In 1999, for example, the *Zagat Survey* reported that the food at a midtown bistro, Patroon, was "better than our ratings show." Yet Tim Zagat claims that he has "virtually never" disagreed with the results of a survey: "If you're a lone dissenter among one hundred, five hundred, or one thousand, you better check your taste buds. That many people are virtually never wrong. I have never felt I had to do an addendum."

Because I had lived in New York, the prospect of becoming regional editor for "the gurus of gourmet" (CNN) rather appealed to my vanity. So I took the job. The brief was simple enough. I was asked to revise a list of twenty-five Dublin restaurants, noting any places that had been redecorated or shut down. I was told to add any restaurants that were, in my opinion, new and noteworthy. After doing that, I was asked to collect some data — opening times, signature dishes, and so on — and write a fifty-word summary for each restaurant. Note the word *summary:* not an actual review, but obviously a reflection of my opinion of the restaurant. I would be paid $50 for each completed data sheet and summary — in most cases, not enough to cover the cost of a single dinner.

I asked for a copy of the 2004 edition, in order to see what format the section would take. Leafing through it, I spotted a couple of blunders and several strange inclusions. I had never heard of one place, another had been shut down by the health inspector, and a third was run by a well-known sociopath.

At the time, I remember wondering if the completed reviews *really* represented the collective opinions of Zagat readers. Still, determined to do a good job, I revisited the restaurants on my list and wrote a fresh review of each. As I was being paid to write about them, I decided that I might as well do the reader and the restaurant justice by providing a new report.

Five months later, the *2005 Zagat Survey* was published. In a bookshop, I read the introduction, written by editor Catherine Bigwood, with mounting pride and a little confusion: "We geared this guide to the upscale international business traveler, soliciting restaurant recommendations from professional food critics in twenty-six major commercial centers. We then asked savvy local diners to rate and review these establishments."

Right, I thought, that is almost logical. They talked to critics *and* consumers. In a separate foreword, on a facing page, Nina and Tim Zagat elucidate:

> This *2005 Europe's Top Restaurants Survey* is an update reflecting significant developments since our last *Survey* was published . . . by regularly surveying large numbers of avid, educated consumers, we hope to have achieved a uniquely current and reliable guide. For this book, 11,258 restaurant-goers from across Europe participated.

All very well, and quite an impressive figure. Imagine a book with eleven *thousand* authors! That moment of giddiness was the high point of my relationship with the *Zagat Survey*. To get a sense of how I felt later that day, after skipping home, book in hand, to read my own contributions, consider the following:

The Review of Chapter One
That Was Printed in the
2004 Zagat Survey

This literary hangout nestled in the vaulted "basement of the Dublin Writers Museum," in a 300-year-old Parnell Square townhouse, draws VIPs for its "great ambiance," "literary décor" and "ancient books" that patrons can peruse; its "sophisticated" Modern European food, the "best Irish coffee in the city" and "attentive service" also make it a bestseller; NB the recent addition of a champagne and oyster bar adds to its shelf life.

My Review of Chapter One
for the *2005 Zagat Survey*

If you're serious about good food and you want a fine-dining experience that is reasonably priced and more casual than Guilbauds, this is where you go. They've revamped the restaurant — at last the loos are cute — so this fine old dining room beneath the Writers Museum now offers ancient style and modern comfort. Try the foie gras, fried egg and black pudding. The charcuterie trolley is legendary. And keep an ear on your neighbours' table. Only four types of people eat at Chapter One: actors, journalists, lawyers and people who sleep with them. All have stories to tell.

The Review of Chapter One
That Was Printed in the *2005 Zagat Survey*

This literary hangout nestled in the vaulted "basement of the Dublin Writers Museum," in a 300-year-old Parnell Square townhouse, draws VIPs for its "great ambiance," "literary décor" and "ancient books" that patrons can peruse; its "sophisticated" Modern European food, the "best Irish coffee in the city" and "attentive service" also make it a bestseller; NB the recent addition of a champagne and oyster bar adds to its shelf life.

It would be unreasonable to expect that all of the information in my review would make it into the guide. However, it did seem peculiar that *none* of the information was used. The review from the previous year's guide had simply been reprinted verbatim. Had 11,258 Zagat readers nothing to say about the city's most popular restaurant? Or were they ignored, like me?

Perhaps that line about the "recent" addition of an oyster bar adding to "its shelf life" was some sort of in-joke. Using the same hot-off-the-press postscript two years in a row, as if the news was just as fresh now, seemed willfully eccentric; could that reference to the long "shelf life" apply not merely to the literary theme of the restaurant, Chapter One, but also to the review itself? A curious joke to play on readers who look to Zagat for "uniquely current" information.

Reading on, I realized that my carefully crafted reviews had been of little or, in most cases, no interest to the editors, who simply reprinted the majority of reviews from the previous edition, making subtle or insignificant changes here and there. Some of the changes were downright cheeky. The 2004 review of one restaurant ended with the words "NB a recent redo may outdate the above score." The following year, the admission had been changed to "NB a post-*Survey* redo may outdate the above score." Where my nominations for new inclusions were accepted, some of the "comments" came only from me, making a nonsense of "consumer" democracy; and when those comments were changed to Zagat-speak, a few meant something quite different. In one case, they were factually incorrect.

I now understand the contempt and respect that rival guides have for one another: if I mentioned Michelin stars in a review, the words "Michelin" and "stars" were excised, but the meaning remained. To put it another way, Zagat editors respect the people at Michelin enough to accept their word when they say a restaurant rocks, but not enough to acknowledge as much in public. The only place where you will find the word "Michelin" is on the back cover, where a plug from *Le Figaro* is reprinted without reference to the context in which it was offered. Everything I now know about the way guidebooks operate makes it hard to believe that the following remark is a compliment: "As good as Michelin."

I could cite other examples of the way in which the Gastronomic Bible, as the *Wall Street Journal* dubs it, is produced, but you probably get the picture by now. Why print old reviews in a guide that claims to be uniquely current? Did the editors think that no one would notice? Perhaps it was just the Dublin section that was so lame? One could hardly describe it as an illustration of Tim Zagat's much-vaunted respect for diners; was it, perhaps, an example of his business nous? I have yet to discover the answer to these questions. As I write, I am still, technically, the regional editor of the *Zagat Survey*.

I guess this means so long.

"So what?" said Arabella, after hearing my account. "You think anyone will find all that surprising?"

"Funny," I replied. "You're the woman who once begged me for a job as a journalist."

"That was before I knew about the French and the Americans and, of course, the bloody English . . ."

"The English?" I said. "Wait a second. I assure you, the English are *not* at fault. You see, when it comes to restaurant criticism . . ."

"Oh, come on," she cried, "don't start that crap."

"OK," I said, rising to the theme, "those hotel guides are not exactly perfect. But I have to tell you, for once, the English are on our side."

"How weird," she replied. "You're a journalist, and for half a second there I actually thought you were being sincere."

6

The English Experience

On Going to Lunch for London

I N 1998, THE PUBLISHER OF *FOOD AND WINE*, KEVIN KELLY, SENT ME to London for a week to help a team of journalists who were writing a guide to the good life. Billed as the ultimate shopping list, *Europe's Elite 1,000* was to be hand delivered to 10,000 of the wealthiest people in the world. A sort of award for being so rich.

The week became six months. I was based in an office on Hans Crescent, opposite Harrods. In a press release, Kevin Kelly claimed that the book would be "compiled with the help and advice of distinguished contributors, celebrities, and individuals of style and substance who were selected for their unique knowledge and excellent local contacts." There is some truth in this claim. We had a small team of journalists and some titled toads whose chief virtue was a knack for getting the best table at San Lorenzo. Being people of the utmost style and sophistication, they never paid for lunch.

The work consisted of writing a short description of companies in the luxury goods sector — and cadging enough free clothes, food, and lodging to sustain the spirit. The firms we championed were supposed to epitomize some rare quality. Resisting the grim tide of mass production, they were pearls, we told readers, in a sea of mediocrity.

Again, there is some truth in this claim. Individually, they remain prestigious brands, but put them together and they read like a list of expensive trademarks: Gucci, Krug, Rolex, Chanel, Versace. When you realize that many of them are controlled by a handful of companies, you wonder if independence, like integrity, has gone out of fashion, or simply underground.

Kevin Kelly hired Sophie, Countess of Wessex, to do the public relations for his new calling card, which had a retail price of $200 and a weight of seven pounds. *Europe's Elite 1,000* had the dual distinction of being the heaviest and most expensive shopping list in history. "Designed to sit on the coffee tables of the finest houses in the world," he wrote, "this book provides a lavish record of the best of the best, from the top florists to the most celebrated restaurants, and the finest galleries to the smartest country clubs." Unfortunately, the book was of little interest to even the newest millionaire. Is there a mogul on the planet who really needs to be told that a crowd called Latour do a rather good claret? Reading the yellow pages of the seriously wealthy is ultimately no different from reading any other phone book. The names intrigue, bore, and, finally, irritate.

I should, of course, be grateful. Kelly brought me to the best restaurants in a city that was then emerging as a culinary superpower. A veteran victim of the Kitchen Con, he also introduced me to the boldest critics working in the language. Even as I separate them from him, by moving on, now, to a short survey of the new food criticism, let me acknowledge Kevin Kelly's determination to eat well by reading every goddamn hack in town. He even put me on to Michael Winner.

It is traditionally said that in continental Europe, people have good food, while the English merely have good table manners. That is perhaps a little misleading, as wealthy Englishmen have eaten well for the last 200 years . . . thanks to great French chefs. The relationship started in 1815 when Antonin Carême was appointed as the Prince Regent's private chef. The regent, who later became King George IV, thought nothing of demanding a banquet with over a hundred courses. Every day for a month.

Carême only stayed two years with the regent, but he established a path that is traveled to this day. In 1841, an English newspaper, *The Globe,* reported that "the man of his age is neither Sir Robert Peel nor Lord John Russell, or even Ibrahim Pasha, but Alexis Soyer." The Parisian was the toast of London before going to the west of Ireland — close, in fact, to Roundstone — where he ran soup kitchens during the Famine. Later, this chef with the soul of a poet went off to the Crimea, where he worked with Florence Nightingale to improve conditions for the troops. The adventure ruined his health and broke his heart. He died shortly after returning to London.

Britain's first restaurant guide, *London at Table,* was published in 1851. Jay Rayner writes:

> There is a description of the Wellington, a restaurant on Piccadilly with two kitchens. One is ruled by a British chef. The other is controlled by "one of the cleverest and most accomplished artistes that Paris can produce." The French menus at the Wellington, which included *consommés, mayonnaise de homard* and *filets de boeuf sauce poivrade,* would remain (depressingly) familiar for more than a century to come.

By the time the chef of kings and king of chefs, Auguste Escoffier, joined forces with César Ritz at the Savoy Hotel in 1890, the upper echelons of London society had already conceded defeat to the French. Like many exponents of the Kitchen Con, Escoffier and Ritz were later sacked for cooking the books. But French chefs remain in the kitchens of England's best restaurants to this day.

In the early years of the twentieth century, most food writing was ponderous, complaisant. Writing in *The Spectator* in 1939, Harold Nicolson struck a rare note of defiance:

> This French invasion of London did immense harm to our national cooking. In place of the fish pies and oyster patties of

coaching days, we entered upon our dining-car period. Even the wet but harmless brill was covered with a pink sauce tinted with cochineal, which in itself is the product of dried beetles from Mexico. We gave up cooking and started to cover up what we had cooked. All flavour having been boiled and roasted out of our foodstuffs, we began replacing it by pungent artificial sauces. Thereafter came the tin age. Indolence allied itself with hearty appetite in order to consummate the defeat of whatever tradition of good cooking may have existed in these islands.

When rationing was introduced during the Second World War, many English people were given their first glimpse of a proper diet. It did not, however, do anything to improve the average English restaurant. Writing in the 1940s, George Orwell noted:

> It is a fact that restaurants which are distinctively English and which also sell good food are very hard to find. Pubs, as a rule, sell no food at all, other than potato crisps and tasteless sandwiches. The expensive restaurants and hotels almost all imitate French cookery and write their menus in French, while if you want a good cheap meal you gravitate naturally towards a Greek, Italian or Chinese restaurant. We are not likely to succeed in attracting tourists while England is thought of as a country of bad food and unintelligible by-laws.

Jay Rayner picks up the story in 1959, when:

> [A] young French chef arrived from the British Embassy in Paris to cook for the renowned Cazalet family in Kent. Four years later, his brother arrived in London to work for the Rothschilds. Their names were Albert and Michel Roux and in 1967 they opened Le Gavroche.

If the Roux brothers hadn't come to Britain, where would British chefs like Pierre Koffman, Rowley Leigh, Gordon Ramsay, Marcus Wareing, and Marco Pierre White have trained?

The Roux brothers dramatically improved the standard of cooking in restaurant kitchens. It is arguable, however, that the greatest influence on the way that Britons dine out today is not a French chef but an Australian publisher. The last thing he made in a kitchen is money, and his name is Rupert Murdoch. At the end of a career spent silencing critics, the Dirty Digger has once again succeeded where no one saw a market, by employing the two most needling journalists in Britain to do the same job for the *same* newspaper. Both enjoy great influence, neither wants to be admired or liked, and together they constitute a threat to the most treasured principles of restaurant criticism.★

The first critic at Murdoch's *Sunday Times* is a vainglorious snob who writes in a prose style that appears to defy logic: everything is staccato, yet still the man cannot stop rambling. Like a cuddly bear with rotten teeth, Michael Winner is just a bit endearing, and the story of his rise to culinary power in Britain is instructive. It proves that *anyone* can become a restaurant critic.

Winner started life as a playboy. Then he became a director. He made over 30 feature films, working with actors like Burt Lancaster, Orson Welles, and Marlon Brando. You may remember the *Death Wish* series, or his 1988 film of Alan Ayckbourn's *A Chorus of Disapproval*. "I'm not a precious theater person," recalls Ayckbourn, "but it wasn't anything I recognized by the time I saw it. I never really told Michael what I thought about it. I just said I didn't want to do anything with him again."

When it became apparent that he was not going to change the direction of cinema, Winner retired to a life of jet-set pranks and long

---

★"Censure," wrote Jonathan Swift, "is the tax a man pays to the public for being eminent." Good critics trade blows with people in the restaurant business. Rupert Murdoch is no stranger to public battle; does this explain his ingenious approach to restaurant criticism? Interviewing the mogul in 2003, Michael Wolff asked: "After holding power in America effectively longer than anyone else in the modern era, what have you learned about being powerful here?" Murdoch dithered for a moment, before muttering, "You make a lot of enemies."

lunches, until an egregious experience prompted him to vent his spleen in the *Sunday Times.* Dining at the Pont de la Tour, "everything was appalling. The food was cold, the service rotten." Winner wrote to the owner of the restaurant, Sir Terence Conran, to record "how a distressing meal had been turned into a remarkably unpleasant evening by the quite extraordinary antics of the unrepentant manager."

"Dear Michael," wrote Sir Terence, "Thank you for your film script. I shall certainly investigate the situation."

Winner's article about the experience provoked such a large response from readers that the editor of the *Sunday Times,* Andrew Neil, decided to ask other luminaries to write reviews. None were so candid, and eventually Neil rang Winner: "I'm fed up with giving these luvvies two hundred quid to say everything's wonderful — what are you doing?" So the "food raconteur" got his column. Millions of people now read it every Sunday to find out where the shameless social climber has been living it up this week, and with whom. Winner is like a dinner-party bore who tells annoyingly good stories. Everyone pretends to have no interest in what he says, but many of us cock an ear. And when he says outrageous things, one can almost hear a nation groan, in a way that is not entirely convincing. There is, after all, something rather endearing about a man who uses his column in a national newspaper to advertise for new girlfriends:

> This is probably the last time you'll read the witty views of Miss Georgina Hristova. Applicants for the vacant position should write in triplicate with their CV and a recent photo. Please list every relationship you've had lasting more than three hours and include your full academic qualifications, although lack of them may not be a problem.

Michael Winner receives more letters than any other journalist at the *Sunday Times.* A few years ago, management contemplated assigning a separate postcode to him, so that mail might be sorted more easily. At the time, a colleague suggested that it was to remove the bile bouquet from everyone else's post. That's not true, of course. Some of the letters are almost sweet.

> Dear Mr. Winner,
> I suspect you may well be as arrogant, pompous, rude and self-opinionated as you come across, but I like you just the same.
>> Yours sincerely,
>> Tony Spear, Oxfordshire

> Dear Sir,
> I'm extremely worried. I used to think Michael Winner was an objectionable, arrogant, conceited individual who threw his money about in the most ostentatious manner. Despite myself, over the past year I've warmed to Mr. Winner. I'm even starting to like him. I admire his stand against the discourtesy of unpunctuality, snooty restaurant staff, rowdy fellow diners and much more. Is there any hope for me?
>> Yours sincerely,
>> Keith Barnes, West Yorkshire

The good news for restaurateurs is that Michael Winner is easy to recognize. He looks like Barbara Cartland. The bad news is that he is remarkably candid and strangely incorruptible. "I'm the only food critic in the world who goes where he wishes to go and pays full price," he boasts. "Nobody else does that. They may pay, but they get it back from the newspaper. I get nothing back from the *Sunday Times*. I pay for the hotels, the food, and I like it that way."

So Winner is untouchable to the PR racket, and impossible to silence. Yes, he has favorites, like all of us, and no, he doesn't make any secret of that fact. But for a man who styles himself as a professional buffoon, Winner is interesting because of his own intolerance of stupidity. It's not that he doesn't suffer fools. He gives them no reason to live.

"What I only go through," wrote Winner of a meal in the Lanesborough Hotel. "How I suffer. The food is grotesque, so awful as to be almost incredible and an absolute disgrace. The owners should call a board meeting at once and fire themselves. And believe me, what I've written so far is kind. Chinese duck cakes turned out to be no more than duck hamburger, with no sauce to help it. It was bland and dreary. For a main course, I ordered a kedgeree of salmon and haddock with curry butter. It was totally uneatable. 'The chef would like to know when your write-up will appear,' the manager said. 'No he wouldn't,' I replied. 'The food is disgusting. I shall say so in no uncertain terms.'"

There is nothing uncommon about a critic who demands some intelligence in a restaurant. Celebrities are among the few critics who dare to make a virtue of their own ignorance. "I don't know much about food," says Michael Winner, "but I know what I like." Readers are prepared to excuse his blunders — he has often complained about the indignity of being served treacle tart that was made without treacle — because he is so entertaining. And his cavalier attitude to facts reveals another truth about the new restaurant criticism. If reviewers truly cared about objectivity, we would employ a host of experts to compensate for our ignorance in certain matters. (What little I know about food dwarfs my knowledge of interior decoration.) Just as one doesn't need a master's in film to critique a movie, anyone with an appetite can review restaurants. Indeed, anyone can become a critic of anything that people are invited to enjoy at a price, and appreciate at one of many levels.

As a critic, you can write about the food, and many readers will praise you, and you can equally devote yourself to the art that hangs on the walls or the draught from the kitchen. Failing that, you can indulge your fondness for anecdotes about Marlon Brando, or reveal the fate of your blind date. In short, as Michael Winner proves, if you have anything vaguely amusing to impart, you can find an audience if you really want one.

Most chefs are not natural writers. In Britain, food critics often know little or nothing about cooking. And if they do, they say that rating a restaurant on the basis of the food is like judging a movie according to the soundtrack. Winner's prominence also belies the myth that good critics eat anonymously (he goes everywhere in a chauffeur-driven 1966 Rolls-Royce Phantom III). The fear that being recognized will compromise your opinion or provide an unfair advantage to the chef is no more rational than hoping he doesn't try to poison you. While a good chef will certainly try that little bit harder when he knows you're a critic, there is no making a genius of a jackass. In the fullness of time — about 15 minutes — all will be revealed.

One day, the critic Matthew Norman was summoned to Michael Winner's $60 million mansion. The sometime film director proved himself a gracious host:

> In the vast drawing room, Michael poured us a delicious Montra-chet ("I was going to give you a really spectacular vintage," he said, having thought better of it), did some pantomime screech-ing at his gardener for our benefit and then gave us the guided tour ... bedroom the size of Bolivia, cinema, underground swimming pool and steam room, the running machine on which he likes to run each morning in the nude.

Winner and Norman went out to review a restaurant called Assaggi in Notting Hill. At the end of his meal, Winner declared that his taglioni with tomato and basil was "very nice, dear."

"Isn't that always the trouble with professional food writers?" asked Norman. "They blind you with technicalities." As Winner pulled away from the curb in his Rolls-Royce, Norman said, "I couldn't find a thing to criticize. Could you?"

"Not enough ice in the Coke, darling."

A. A. Gill, the second critic at Murdoch's *Sunday Times,* used to work for Michael Winner — as his gardener. Today, he drives a Mountain Dew–colored Bentley. Like Winner, he is banned from several restaurants, and he is the only other journalist who is capable of starting an argument in the office on Monday morning.

Battling a marathon drug habit, Adrian Gill once taught a ten-day cooking class for men who wanted to seduce women. In the early 1970s, he ran a pornographic bookshop in Soho. Then he became a drug dealer. "I got on my bike and sold dope and speed and coke and pills out of people's mothers' cabinets ... It was selling drugs that got me where I am today." Dyslexic, and sober for over twenty years, Gill files his copy by reading it aloud to editors over the phone. The man who put the rant in restaurant, his columns are composed of broadsides, iconoclastic aperçus, and withering remarks about his girlfriend, The Blonde. There is often some mention of the meal itself.

"I turned to journalism," says Gill, "because it was the only thing left for me to do."

Writing in *Vanity Fair* recently, Gill savaged 66, then the hottest new restaurant in Manhattan. The review was the talk of polite society, and the curse of every chef. One told a newspaper, "He wanted to go to the busiest restaurant in Manhattan and fuck it up." Given the amount of publicity the restaurant received, this assertion is open to question. I just tried to book a table for next Friday night. Waiting list. Probably just as well:

> How clever are shrimp-and-foie-gras dumplings with grapefruit dipping sauce? What if we called them fishy liver-filled condoms? . . . They were properly vile, with a savor that lingered like a lovelorn drunk and tasted as if your mouth had been used as the swab in an animal hospital.

Adrian Gill has power, wit, contempt for orthodox thinking, a love of food, and a brain that is bigger than Birmingham. Chefs hate him, as do critics; indeed, many of Gill's readers would sooner be rid of him. Until, that is, he goes. In the meantime, he is one of the world's most influential restaurant critics.

"If the food is the star of your meal," says Gill, "you're eating with the wrong people."

Until a few years ago, such a claim was rarely made. Today, it is widely accepted as fact, and not simply among restaurant critics. When was the last time you went out for dinner? It might have been an intimate supper, a groping affair in some candle-lit cavern? Was it a meeting of like minds, old friends, new love, or some business with a client? Do you remember the moment when you arrived? Were you hungry? Tired? Did you sit in the heart of the dining room or just outside the bathroom? These things matter because, unlike the food, they usually inform our opinion of a restaurant.

In 2003, Professor John Edwards of Bournemouth University served an identical dish, chicken à la king, to customers in ten different dining rooms. Edwards discovered that the better the ambience, the better the food tasted. The dish was given low marks in a residential nursing home and a boarding school and got top marks at a four-star restaurant.

Expectation and ambience inform our opinion of dinner; so do plaudits. In a 1999 review of Charlie Palmer's New York restaurant Aureole, William Grimes of the *New York Times* christened the Zagat Effect. Simply put, the more you're told how good it is, the more you'll enjoy yourself in a restaurant. So a couple of Michelin stars or a rave review in the Zagat guide will send thousands of hungry sheep to dinner on the other side of town, and a great night out is guaranteed, even if the chef has lost the will to live.

Why the World Needs Food Critics

In 2004, a psychologist, J. J. Goode, asked sixty-one students to taste a cheese for three days in a row. Each day, the cheese was the same, but the participants were told that it was variously cheddar, supermarket-brand cheddar, and award-winning cheddar. Their opinions changed dramatically each day. Goode writes on egullet.com:

From this experiment, I drew two tentative conclusions. The first is that expectations do play a role in subsequent taste evaluations. The second is that there is nothing wrong with letting the judgments and suggestions of others guide your gustatory preferences. Norway rats develop some of their food preferences by sniffing the excrement of other rats, to tell what they ate. Humans, with their distinctive capacity for complex language, express their food preferences in newspapers and magazines.

Writing in the *Observer Food Monthly,* the chef Nigel Slater acknowledges a seismic shift in the culture of criticism:

> One of the hallmarks of a good restaurant critic is that they avoid describing every last mouthful of food in boorish detail. They let us know they have found somewhere we might like to spend our hard-earned cash (or not) and we learn to trust their judgment. The most entertaining critics also seem to be the ones who regularly go off-piste and simply amuse or infuriate us as well as telling us about what they ate. In short, we value the writing as much as the opinions.

Is the life of a critic demanding? Self-styled epicures — French or American — conceal their own ignorance and dress up the significance of their "research." In the Age of Appetite, there is a new breed of reviewer: candid, biased, British, and no great friend of cordon bleu. Meet Giles Coren of *The Times,* a newspaper that was once regarded as a bastion of traditional values★: "Is it hard to be a restaurant critic? Actually, it's a piece of piss."

So life as a critic is one long holiday in the land of Arctic char tartare. And what about objectivity? It must, for sure, be difficult to operate in a market with so many rivals. Do you take the opinion of the menu-maulers into account? Or do you try to be impartial? Until very recently, critics didn't even talk about this sort of thing. "I gave E&O a crap review," says Coren, "because Adrian Gill loved it."

When he was voted Food and Drink Writer of the Year at the British Press Awards in 2005, Coren took the opportunity to reveal his modus operandi:

> If the first restaurant I select is an absolute hummer, I just ignore it and try somewhere else. And if the second one is equally minging, well, then, I have no option but to roll my sleeves up and tuck into one of those embarrassing table-thumpers of mine, full

---

★It is now owned by Rupert Murdoch.

of unnecessary ad hominem ranting and similes that begin with a plate of food and end with a witty word for faeces.

To confirm his interest in matters lavatorial, Coren devotes 300 words of the same review to a description of a man urinating in front of the restaurant window.

Writing in the *New York Times* in 2004, Warren St. John conceded that British critics are far more truculent than those in France or America. "They don't give chefs a few months to hit their stride, but instead show up on opening night, as on Broadway. They don't go incognito, but rather appear under their own names, often with a pack of friends, sometimes expecting star treatment."

In New York, the restaurant press could not be less aggressive. In London, the cacophony of irate voices feeds a culture in which critics race to newly opened restaurants in order to review them before anyone else. And in their haste to arrive at the scene of a triumph — or an accident — the dogs of dinner dispense with niceties. Even Fay Maschler is not above the occasional hatchet job. "It is difficult, if not impossible," she wrote of one experience, "to imagine anyone conjuring up a restaurant, even in their sleep, where the food in its mediocrity comes so close to inedible." (In other words, the lawyers would not let her say that it *was* inedible.) The put-down princess won her job as the *Evening Standard* restaurant critic in a competition in 1972. Thirty-three years later, Maschler revealed some of the abuse she regularly receives:

> The first threat of a lawsuit I received came from a restaurant proprietor who didn't seem to realise that the rules can change. He was outraged that the pastiche French food he had bullied his customers into believing was the real thing could be criticised. And by a woman. The world of chefs and restaurateurs is a male-dominated place, a sort of minor public school where the ability to browbeat counts for a lot . . . Luke Johnson (ex-owner of The Ivy and Le Caprice) once asked, "What moral right does a restaurant critic have to make judgements?" I say, "What moral right do some restaurateurs have to trade unchecked while inflicting on the public mediocre food unprofessionally served?"

Matthew Norman's reviews are best read after lunch, as they don't exactly fuel the appetite (noodle-flavored mullet, chicken à la iron filings). The last time I read a rave review by him, the place in question had the bad fortune to go out of business on the day before the piece appeared. Norman is the man whom Richard Shepherd threatened to sue, after the critic wrote:

> Where do you start with somewhere like Shepherds? You don't. If you have any sense, you finish with it. There is so much about Shepherds that is wrong that it would, in a more elegant age, merit a pamphlet rather than a review.

"These statements are a vicious rant," said Mr. Shepherd, who later described the critic as "a guileless, mean, uncharitable, miserable old two-bit scribbler."

The Observer's Jay Rayner has written a novel called The Apologist, about a food critic whose harsh review provokes a chef to commit suicide. Rayner denies that it is based on personal experience but does admit that several victims have proposed "doffing me up down a dark alley." In 2001, a Labour MP, Tom Watson, memorably described the critic as "a flatulent oaf." That was the year in which Rayner wrote the following account of a restaurant in Glasgow:

> The old Sheriff's Court is now a place where the crimes are actually committed. Granted, bad cooking probably does not warrant a long stretch inside. But the offence of grievous bodily harm upon a lovely little sea bream really ought to carry with it some form of judicial penalty. There was no cutlery on our table. I looked for waiting staff, but the room is so big they were probably obscured by the curvature of the Earth. Eventually we got up and nicked knives and forks off a table half a kilometre away. It was a bit of a pity we did, because it meant we could eat.

The boom in criticism, which was largely provoked by Gill and Winner, has changed the context in which lunch is assessed. While chefs will always moan, readers love it when the knives are drawn — when Matthew Norman had his little altercation with Richard Shepherd, it was headline news for several days — and as editors acknowledge the pulling power of an iconoclast, more work is made available to new voices. Putative critics should welcome this development. Inevitably, however, some new recruits are rather too giddy to survive the slings and arrows for long. James Major is the son of former prime minister John Major. The following extract is from Master Major's first review in the *Daily Telegraph:*

> As many of my friends know, I am not a great lover of fancy food. That's not to say I don't like food — I love it . . . but I know what I like and I most certainly know what I don't like. As much as I enjoy wine, I prefer chilled lager, so we ordered two halves of lager. Then the main course arrived. It may appear strange to order two chicken curries from a restaurant such as The Ivy, but when my fiancée, Emma, and her friend tucked into them, it was clear that curry was absolutely the right choice.

Startling competitiveness is the most obvious evidence of a boom in restaurant reviewing. The emergence of ultra-candid criticism, ostensibly to stand out from the crowd, has created a fiercely partisan scene in which bitter disagreement is the norm rather than the exception. So A. A. Gill can describe San Lorenzo as "quite the worst restaurant in London, maybe the world," while Craig Brown thinks it's "the sort of restaurant you hope to stumble upon in Rome or in Florence, and about which you thank your lucky stars. It is immediately glamorous, fun, special and so whole-heartedly Italian that at the end of the evening walking back into Knightsbridge came as something of a shock."

Gill was equally shocked by San Lorenzo, in a rather different way:

> They serve horrendous food, grudgingly, in a dining room that is a museum to Italian waiters taste circa 1976. It's laughably overpriced, but doesn't take credit cards. But all that is just by the by compared with its unique horror. To get in, you have to be kissed

by a woman called Mara, who must surely have been around to do tongues with Garibaldi.

One may regard this competitiveness as slightly juvenile, or even irresponsible. The feeding frenzy, more democratic than a heavily censored press, also has the virtue of being efficient. Competition serves the public by arming diners with information. If it is wildly contradictory, that is not, perhaps, a comment on criticism but on the experience of dining in restaurants: too various to reflect one opinion. The hard-boiled dregs of the restaurant racket, most London critics operate in a murky, imprecise way, and they are often too cruel. Like a friend who calls to say bad luck or an ex who says how well you look, the best sometimes leave us wondering what their motives really are. In the end, however, we think them strangely faithful.

It is tempting, but wrong, to conclude that the new candor of British restaurant criticism is a function of some change in the definition of libel. Age has something to do with it. Many of the newly prominent English critics belong to a generation that knows the taste of everything, and how to cook nothing. They dine out all the time, and thus feel entitled to air their views on the subject. They also venerate personal opinion. This reflects a larger shift within popular culture. When the American author James Frey confessed that large parts of his bestselling memoir, *A Million Little Pieces,* were fabricated or wildly embellished, literary critic Michiko Kakutani noted:

> Cable news is now peopled with commentators who serve up opinions and interpretation instead of news, just as the Internet is awash in bloggers who trade in gossip and speculation instead of fact. For many of these people, it's not about being accurate or fair. It's about being entertaining, snarky or provocative — something that's decidedly easier and less time-consuming to do than old-fashioned investigative reporting or hard-nosed research.

Until recently, there was a lively debate in Britain about the blurring of the boundary between hard news and hard views. The "respectable" end of the trade — in other words, the BBC and one or two broadsheets — presumed the moral high ground, while most tabloids seemed to regard facts as meddlesome. The Iraq war (more specifically, the actions of figures such as Andrew Gilligan and Piers Morgan) changed all that. Today, there is less talk of ethical distinctions between "good" and "bad" journalism. Rather, there is a new scepticism. As John Lloyd writes in his book *What the Media Are Doing to Our Politics:* "Many journalists don't believe in the existence of truth — and certainly believe that, even if it does exist, it is unattainable by journalism." That concession, coupled with the enshrinement of subjectivity as a supreme virtue within the culture, helps us to understand why writing on food, once the preserve of gentleman cooks and Chelsea matrons — the bookish cooks of earnest broadsheets — is now regarded by newspaper editors as a crude but effective weapon in the battle to boost circulation.

Cultural commentators are entitled to question the ascendancy of the first-person singular. In the world of restaurant criticism, it has been a good thing. Competition raises the bar for critics *and* chefs, ensuring that diners are taken more seriously. There is, I believe, a connection between better criticism and a rejuvenated restaurant industry. That may explain why *Gourmet* has declared that London is the restaurant capital of the world. "A few years ago, the food was no better than bad American food," said the magazine's executive editor, John Willoughby, in May 2005. "Now, when people ask me where to go, I tell them 'London.' The glory days are back."*

---

*While London is hailed as a foodie paradise, there are vast swathes of Britain in which provender comes from a microwave oven. And the great English dish of the day, every day, is chicken tikka masala. There are more Indian restaurants in London than Mumbai. When an American reporter asked Sting what his hometown of Newcastle was like, he replied, "It's a nice place to bring up your food." Also, it is not the small number of Michelin masterpieces that make a city special, nor the antics of its celebrity chefs. The quality and profusion of small neighbourhood restaurants reveals more than any claim made for headlines. On that basis, London's preeminence is open to debate: Sydney or New York could also claim the title of restaurant capital. Let's not forget that, despite its woes, Paris is full of great restaurants for *all* budgets, while the culinary heritage of Italy is arguably richer than anywhere else.

★ ★ ★

There is a connection here — customer, critic and chef are closer than all imagine — and also the hint of an opportunity. Most reviewers last six or seven years. There may be half a dozen distinctive voices where you live, and possibly one who deserves a bigger stage. Another stage waits for someone with the chutzpah to fill it. The world's most venerable collection of restaurant criticism has never seemed so redundant. "Michelin is an absurd and pointless system," says A. A. Gill. "It's an irrelevance," says chef Alastair Little, "and it ignores the best food in Britain." No one has forged a global standard in restaurant criticism.

Humans are more demanding and more discerning than at any point in history. The Age of Appetite presents new challenges, as well as an opportunity: to put sense on truth, or free it from decades of phoney dogma. In the world of haute cuisine, there is still too much of the latter and not enough truth for one decent conversation. The English are trying to change all that.

In October 1999, Kevin Kelly sent me to New York to explore the possibility of replicating the apparent success of *Europe's Elite 1,000* in America. This was all part of an elaborate empire-building exercise that I still don't understand. In time, if all went according to plan, the publisher would also produce a coffee-table book that listed the names of most of the rich and powerful Jews around the world. The idea was "to create a tasteful and enduring commemoration of the Jewish contribution to contemporary society." I spent a few weeks researching that book. It was a fascinating project until the day it emerged that a lot of neo-Nazi Web sites already feature such a list. After that, it all felt rather tasteless.

Kelly has never had a shortage of big ideas. The Irishman had made several million dollars when he sold *The World of Interiors* to Condé Nast, and he achieved critical success with a beautiful, ill-fated magazine for Irish-Americans, *The World of Hibernia*. He created *Departures* for American Express, and *Business,* with the *Financial Times* and Condé Nast as partners. Now he wanted to create a social climbers' manual in the one great power that has consistently rejected snobbery as a tool of the *ancien régime.*

But Kelly didn't see it like that. "Sophisticated Europeans are visiting the United States in greater numbers than ever before," he wrote in 1997. "They come to buy businesses and to shop on Madison Avenue or Rodeo Drive. They ski in Aspen, take a house in the Hamptons, play golf at Augusta and visit the wineries of the Napa Valley."

In other words, the action had moved west. So, in a shameless attempt to pave the way for his glorious return, the publisher sent me off to take Manhattan. My target was the *very* new rich: the sort of people who had yet to realize that winning a lottery is lucky, not chic. They, after all, were the only readers who had liked the European version of the *Elite 1,000.* And they were the people who fascinated Kevin Kelly.

"This is the big one," he said one night; the voice of a man made rich from unlikely adventures. "I'm heading uptown, and you're going to open the door."

"Perhaps Monsieur would care for something more expensive?"

7

Celebrity Chefs

Starring Gordon Ramsay and Conrad Gallagher

A CERTAIN SORT OF CHEF REQUIRES SPECIAL ATTENTION. HE IS found in all countries with kitchens that are large enough to accommodate a TV camera, hair, makeup, and an oversized ego, and wherever women think that a man who cooks should be encouraged, no matter how foul or abusive he is when sober. Why, he will wonder, have I not been celebrated for all that I have done? And when, he must wonder, will this book get around to heralding my ascension?

In the idiom of the subject: shut up, Gordon, your hour has come.

To become a celebrity chef in England, it is essential to have some cursory skills in the kitchen, a big mouth, and a deep, abiding belief in the proposition that there is no such thing as bad publicity. It helps to have a really hostile personality. You need to upset your wife, your staff, and the guy from *The Times* on table three. You want your rivals to hate you, for a man among his mates is a schmuck at this end of the market. They should be talking about you from Babington House in Somerset to the Bel Air Hotel in Los Angeles. And when the last great scorer comes to write against your name, you should probably tell him to fuck off.

In America, celebrity chefs are less exotic, if just as pompous. They are quite mad enough to think that AIDS is caused by OXO, and they also believe that truffles are the cure for any disease. Loud enough to brag but too coy to slate a rival, they front television shows and lend a name to saucepans. In England, editors would send them home to mother for a hug and a nice cup of tea.

In the infinitely peculiar world of the English celebrity chef, bad behavior is encouraged, and an exotic social life is a bonus. (That's not feta cheese; it's a block of cocaine.) Our hero is usually pictured leaving a nightclub with a bottle of Cristal in one hand and a model in the other. This pale simulation of glamour is made all the more ludicrous by the truth. The celebrity chef has a steady supply of potential backers, each hungry to invest in some dodgy new "concept." Few can stand the heat for long, getting out of the kitchen with two burned fingers and a firm resolve to lose money elsewhere in future.

Naturally, we are going to concentrate on exceptions to these rules. Mavericks are always more interesting than archetypes. For example, the *enfant terrible* of British restaurants, Marco Pierre White, does not even bother with cooking anymore. Having reached the pinnacle of culinary greatness, with several restaurants and a daily tabloid mug shot, White now gets his kicks elsewhere. When he's not getting up at four o'clock in the morning to go shooting with his Japanese butler, this Renaissance man oversees a range of "innovative convenience meals." "It is about giving the nation access to good food," he says, without apparent irony.

Marco Pierre White's crown has been passed to his protégé, a man made bitter by success. Gordon Ramsay has three Michelin stars, a bag of chips on either shoulder — and audacious plans to open restaurants in Manhattan, Boca Raton, and Los Angeles. Shame about that ego. The *New York Times* recently described Ramsay as "culinary virtuoso cum footballer thug." As the following comments prove, celebrity chefs are no less petulant than a rich young woman who can't find any more heroin. Ramsay on White:

Marco — that was the greatest shame to me, having worked for him for that level of time, and admired him, and striving for that level of perfection. I don't know how he didn't want to sustain it for a longer period. He's a great chef but he's stopped playing. Great footballers never make great managers . . . when you listen to Marco's philosophy, you've got to question: is it in the interests of him or the interests of you? Because Marco now, as opposed to being Britain's best chef, is Britain's number one manipulator. His manipulation now is better than his cooking.

When Madonna tried to book a table for ten people in one of Ramsay's restaurants, he responded by telling her personal assistant, "I don't care who the fuck she is. We don't do tables for ten. My largest table is a six." The assistant asked him if Ramsay would cook in the singer's hotel suite for $10,000. He said, "No, because I'm not a prostitute."

Even Lynn Barber, a legendary British journalist, found it difficult to put some sense on this awkward Scot:

He is difficult to interview because he can't really sit still, he talks tabloidese, hops from subject to subject and delivers his insults in a flail of punches instead of with one smooth, deadly stiletto strike. It is dangerous to mention the f words — failed footballer — in his company, but that is what he is, a Glasgow Rangers footballer to boot. And his face and manner are still far more suggestive of Ibrox Park than Claridges.

When A. A. Gill brought Joan Collins to dinner at Ramsay's new restaurant in that famous hotel, the chef came out, shook their hands, and muttered, "I want you to leave." So they did. Twenty minutes later, a journalist from the *Daily Mail* rang Gill, inquiring about the incident: "Mr. Gill, we've had a call from Gordon Ramsay. Would you like to comment?" One must admire that nerve. Here was one of the most celebrated chefs in Britain, trying to extract publicity for throwing Joan Collins out of his restaurant, by inventing a fight between himself and a critic who had praised his cooking. Referring to the incident in the *Sunday Times,* Gill wrote that Ramsay had turned it into a publicity stunt. "He said he was pleased it was the first restaurant I'd been thrown out of, because it was like losing your virginity, which tells you a lot about his attitude to sex."

Three months later, Ramsay closed Amaryllis in his hometown of Glasgow. The chef had previously claimed that there wasn't a demand for high-quality food in Scotland, which may not have impressed his customers. Noting that people in London are more affected by the cult of celebrity chefs, Edinburgh restaurateur Juliet Lawrence Wilson told a newspaper, "Food critics go gaga over someone like Gordon Ramsay coming here, whereas the public don't. And then there's the fact that he's not working in the restaurant. Why should people be impressed by his name when he's not even there?"

"There are many things he could have done to save the restaurant," noted one member of Ramsay's staff. "Being there would have been a bloody start."

The following week, after, one assumes, another meeting with his bank manager, Ramsay shut the doors on Fleur in Mayfair, which had only been open for six months. Richard Harden, coauthor of the respected Harden's guide, told a newspaper at the time:

> He was opening restaurants that people were going to on the strength of the Gordon Ramsay name, as opposed to the inherent quality of the restaurants themselves. He clearly was and is an excellent name, but was at risk of diluting it by trading on it. Even Gordon Ramsay can't be in two places at once.

In a show of defiance, Ramsay — ever the showman — then embarked on filming yet another television show. With names like *Boiling Point, Cutting the Mustard,* and *Faking It,* what links these programs (apart from the dodgy titles) is the fact that they test the limits of good taste. It is not that Ramsay is bad for television; the camera loves him, and he loves it. The man obviously has charisma. And he may well be the greatest chef that Britain has ever produced. But his face, language, and manners are deeply offensive to anyone with a modicum of sensitivity. The difference between Gordon Ramsay and a talking pig is that Gordon Ramsay never shuts up.

Ramsay's New York venture, which opened at a cost of $6 million in November 2006, is housed on the ground floor of the London Hotel. The chef claimed before the opening that he would spend ten-day stints there, with three-day breaks in London, "at least until the new year." And he promised to treat his staff with respect. "I've already been warned," he said at the time of the opening. "The moment I touch down at the airport, I get put in my straitjacket and I go straight to my management skills to learn how to ask a kitchen porter to wash out a copper pan for me."

The only thing that Gordon Ramsay likes more than food is publicity. In 2004 he posed naked — plus conger eel — on the cover of the *Sunday Times* style section, the home of A. A. Gill. Asked whether the photo shoot was a challenge, Ramsay replied, "What, a conger round my donger? Yes, a challenge, a rush. I was thinking about my oxtail while I was doing it, infusing it with cardamon pods so we get a rich red-wine sauce for the sea bass tomorrow. Cheap oxtail and the sumptuous Rolls-Royce of fish, the delicate against the robust."

There has never been any doubt about Ramsay's dedication to food. He used to sleep in the dining room of one of his restaurants, and he even malaprops in the language of the kitchen: "It's strange walking up to Claridges," he told one interviewer, "and seeing your name on the restaurant canapé." But posing naked with a conger eel? That outlandish bid for yet more publicity suggests that cooks are the hungriest hookers of all. It also represents a bizarre riposte to A. A. Gill, who claimed a few weeks before the photo shoot that "celebrity chefs are the most immoderate graspers of limelight. They will crawl naked over live lobsters for a flashbulb."

That sounds like an obituary for Ireland's most famous chef. The demise of Conrad Gallagher has often been noted. Like Gordon Ramsay (who is, he says, "a fabulous guy"), Gallagher has talent, an exotic personality, and a habit of walking away. His fame neatly bookends the beginning and end of the Celtic Tiger, the boom that made Ireland one of the most successful economies in the world. But the real story of Conrad Gallagher has not yet been written.

This rural Icarus was born in the wilds of County Donegal in 1971. He started washing dishes in Bundoran at the age of fifteen. Two years later, he went to New York, where he quickly landed a prepping job in Queens. One night, the manager of the Plaza Hotel happened to be dining in the restaurant. Gallagher was hired on the spot. After a stint at the Plaza, he became the youngest ever sous-chef at Peacock Alley in the Waldorf Astoria Hotel.

Setting a pattern, Conrad moved on quickly.

After six months at the Hotel de Paris, Alain Ducasse's three-star shrine in Monte Carlo, Gallagher arrived back in Ireland and opened his own Peacock Alley — a steal that will never be punished. After a couple of false starts, the restaurant found a home in a hotel in the center of Dublin. With his velvet-rope social life and big mouth, Gallagher was a darling, and later a demon, of the gossip columns. He drip-fed hacks the lurid details of a life that Jeffrey Archer could mine for good material.

"I had expensive tastes," says Gallagher today, with memorable understatement. "The Gucci, the really nice clothes, the fancy handbags. I knew that was the lifestyle I wanted." That extravagance was evident in the restaurant, where he spent $2,000 on flowers for the reception area and insisted on having his fish delivered by taxi.

In 1997, Gallagher won a Michelin star. The award surprised those who had dared to question the chef's opinion of himself and his fancy handbags. I was banned from Peacock Alley after writing an ambivalent review. Gallagher was incensed that a local hack might doubt his genius, as if it weren't abundantly obvious. A few weeks later, I met him in a nightclub, sandwiched between Bono and his Boswells (I had even less reason to be there than Gallagher). After a little flirting with some rock-star wives and several trips to the bathroom, Gallagher appeared to acknowledge my presence. Leaning over, he shouted in my ear, "You know, your brother's got a lot to learn." But Conrad doesn't know my brother.

"And so do you," I said.

At the time, the great young hope had many fans in the press. "No one else cooks like Conrad Gallagher," wrote John McKenna, my predecessor at the *Irish Times,* "because no one else can cook like Conrad Gallagher. This is food as theatre. Thrilling. Outrageous. Unique." And *very* expensive.

Gallagher expanded rapidly, and within a few months it was difficult to walk into a Dublin restaurant without encountering one of his architectural follies. That was partly because his cooking has always been imitated (if chefs are artists, why do most have no imagination?) and partly because Conrad was all over the place: at one point, he had six restaurants. Then there was the newspaper column, the TV show, the four cookbooks, the cooking school and the bar back home in sleepy Donegal. As if to advertise the owner's delusions, it was called The Metropolitan.

Most chefs are poor businessmen, and while he thrived for a year or two, Gallagher was no exception. "Conrad was like a graceful swan on the surface," says one admirer, "but down below he was paddling furiously to stay afloat." He became, by his own admission, an Antichrist, working twenty-two hours a day. Then he was struck with cancer. Twice. It all proved too much. The creditors moved in, Gallagher buckled, and five restaurants shut within three months. Ultimately, he was sunk by lawyers, but not before hurting real people. How did our hero feel? Remorseful? Angry? "My personal life crumbled."

Dublin proved too small for the debt-ridden chef, and his ego demanded a larger audience. So he fled to London. Turning on the charm, Gallagher convinced an Irish entrepreneur, Vince Power, to back a large new restaurant on Shaftesbury Avenue. With typical restraint, our hero called it Restaurant Conrad Gallagher. Bill Clinton was among the first customers. A few months later, the chef's contract was terminated after "financial irregularities" emerged at the restaurant.

At the time, the police were reportedly "anxious" to talk to Gallagher about the disappearance of cash and fittings from the restaurant. However, no charges have been brought.

In 2002, Vince Power said of Gallagher, "If he ever sets foot in England again, I will bankrupt him." One supplier said the chef was the worst client he has had in twenty years of business. Just when it looked as if things couldn't get sloppier, Gallagher's landlord in Dublin initiated legal action to recover three paintings from Peacock Alley, which the chef had sold for $20,000.

"I have enemies," said Gallagher in June 2002. "But I'm not afraid of meeting them." He was in New York at the time, where he quickly fell in love, got "married" to an American, and opened a fashionable new bar and restaurant. At the time, I predicted that he would become a New York legend:

> If his reputation is in tatters at home, where does Conrad Gallagher go now? Nowhere. He's staying in New York, with his new restaurant and new wife. She's about to give birth to a green card. The city will lap up his talent and his energy. Americans are more forgiving, or America is bigger.

In April 2003, two weeks after hosting the after-show party for the MTV Awards, Gallagher was arrested in his restaurant. He spent six weeks in the Brooklyn Detention Center, awaiting extradition to Ireland on charges of stealing the three paintings from Peacock Alley. At his first hearing, Gallagher asked to address the court. "Just regarding the jumping the bail," he muttered, "I didn't really jump."

A Legal Aid lawyer stuck a notepad in front of his client's face and pulled him away from the bench. "I think," he spluttered, "my client wants to exercise his right to remain silent."

Gallagher was extradited to Ireland, where sympathizers put forward money to ensure his release on bail. He used the money to pay his legal fees and made $20,000 by selling a story about "Cooking for the Godfather in America's Most Notorious Prison." His own father put up a $60,000 bail bond to get the chef out of jail. Recently, one of those sympathizers who lent money to secure his release said, "I don't know him that well but I didn't want to see him in prison. I thought the money was for his bail, so I would get it back whether he got off the charges or not. I didn't expect to have to go looking for the money back. Now he's gone to South Africa and I can't get through to him. His number has changed."

Gallagher won the case, although the hotel still refused to admit that the paintings had been his to sell. Eventually, after threats of further legal action, Gallagher dropped his claim to the paintings, and his old landlord, the Fitzwilliam Hotel, donated them to charity.

At the time of writing, Conrad Gallagher is living in Cape Town, where he commands a $200,000 salary and the honor of being South Africa's only Michelin-starred cook. As a consultant to a chain of five-star hotels, he oversees kitchens in Durban, Botswana, and Swaziland. Back in Ireland, he still makes headlines, most recently after his latest wedding, when a jilted ex accused him of bigamy.

"It's a gift," says Vince Power, who is still owed "a fucking fortune." "He has the ability to win a following wherever he goes. I've seen him in company and people are in awe of him . . . He's his own worst enemy. He could have been the biggest celebrity chef in Britain, but he kept pressing the self-destruct button."

Gallagher could have been Ramsay. An uncomfortable emblem of Ireland's Golden Age, his story serves as a warning to those who would fly too close to the sun. But the obituaries are premature. At thirty-five, Ireland's most notorious chef is still young. There is only one man who can write the next chapter of this singular tale. His name is Conrad Gallagher.

8

The Waiting Game

Reflections on the Value of Service

I ONCE SPENT A SUMMER WORKING AS A WAITER ON THE ISLAND OF Bermuda. Like a lot of sleepy, once-chic hotels, Newstead was full of poor couples on honeymoon, rich couples on their second honeymoon, and furtive couples on fictional business trips. I had good fun flirting with all the nice new wives, but adulterers were much better tippers. Every morning after breakfast, I would scurry off to the tennis court for an hour or two, before lunch service began. After lunch, I would head into Hamilton on a moped. There, I would trawl the capital's charity shops, looking for billionaire's garbage. My wardrobe is still full of dead-man blazers and faded pink polo shirts.

I tell you these things by way of preface to a chapter that is full of rebuke and admonition. I am angry, you see, about the way diners are treated in restaurants. But you may as well know where I'm coming from: on the day he sacked me, the manager described me as the second-worst waiter he had ever met.

Mark you, it is perhaps more accurate to describe the parting as a court-martial. I was a bitter disappointment to the maître d', an ex-general in the Yugoslav army who now ran the dining room like a prisoner-of-war camp. Guests were greeted in broken English, for no less than nine seconds and no more than fifteen, and their predilections were noted in capital letters on a blackboard in the kitchen. On the day that guests/prisoners left/escaped, waiters were forbidden from shaking hands with them; only the general could benefit from any largesse.

I was hired on the basis that a young Irishman called Barry McGuigan had recently distinguished himself in the boxing ring. I must have some of McGuigan's vim, reasoned the maître d.' (As preconceptions go, this is no more offensive than assuming that Germans are all mustachioed megalomaniacs.) I was pleased to prove the Yugoslav wrong. However, with the passing of time it becomes easier to see him in a benign light. I recall, for instance, that it wasn't my incompetence that distressed the general, but rather my habit of speaking with the customers at length. To me, it was perfectly natural to inquire about the size of the fish that got away, or the length of the gash on the side of Sir's arm after falling off his moped again. When Madam made familiar remarks about my freckles, to the evident disgust of Sir, it seemed apposite to respond by winking. This tactic for adding to the gaiety of the island was inevitably considered a success the following morning, when Sir and Madam wore bashful smiles. There is no better prelude to great sex than a good argument.

The highlight of my short career as a waiter was the discovery of a $100 bill underneath a teacup. I have never had an opportunity to thank the New Yorker who left the tip, and I trust that he is reconciled with his wife. I now recall his silent kindness, as well as my short, ill-fated stint in silver service, and when I reflect on the reality of waiting tables, it is easy to imagine a world in which we are all just doing our best.

Then I think of dinner last night.

"All I've got is my career," says Rebecca, the waitress on *Cheers,* "and I don't like it." She is not alone. History teaches us that at some dim point in the past, humans regarded service as a noble calling. Today, in terms of the level of esteem that society affords it, working in a restaurant is just below clerking in a video store and just above selling cocaine. The art of running a dining room is practiced in the main by resting actors and middle-class dropouts. Neither have much interest in other human beings, and both have reason to be deeply insecure.

CUSTOMER: Any sign of those mains?

WAITRESS: Honey, I'm not the chef; I'm just a waitress. And to tell you the truth, I'm really an actress.

CUSTOMER: Good. Why don't you *act* like a waitress?

Was it always like this, or did service once begin with a capital S? The memory plays tricks on us all. So the halcyon recollection of a summer picnic will not include the washing up and rain, and a dazzling soufflé will forever taste fresh in the memory; do you remember how long you waited for it? On the other hand, as Flaubert noted, ignorance of history makes us vilify our own age. So we readily lament a decline in standards on the spurious basis that they were higher at some point in the past.

Restaurant standards have consistently improved over the last hundred years, and an unprecedented number of people are now discovering how enjoyable it is to devour good food made by strangers. However, there is one crucial respect in which standards are dropping, and there is very little we can do about it. The service in our restaurants reflects a wider phenomenon: the demise of ritual, and the rise of informality.

In 1976, a reader of *The Times* wrote to the editor:

I used to go to a certain restaurant for years and years. And I always had the same waiter and I always said to him, "How are you today?" and he always replied, "Good of you to ask, Sir." Then one day he suddenly started telling me how he was, and I realised that a whole way of life had changed. The formality had been spoiled, and of course it was an awful bore because one did not really want to know.

Ignore the risible snobbery: there is a useful observation here. Decorum is supposed to be part of the job. When Marian Scrutton accepted an award as the Host of the Year in Britain, she said, "In France and Italy, being a waiter is regarded as a profession. In this country, there is no recognition of the skills a waiter has to possess, and consequently no self-esteem among them."

Spike Milligan once wrote a couplet that summarizes the relationship between diner and server in a country where equality remains a thorny issue.

> "What will you have?" said the waiter, pensively picking his nose.
>   "I'll have two boiled eggs, you bastard. You can't put your fingers in those."

All over the United Kingdom, surly young men in dirty black loafers think the class system is still holding them down. You, diner, are doing your bit to perpetuate injustice, and that is why you deserve to be treated like the enemy. Contrast that attitude with the enthusiasm and friendliness of American staff, who are often more anxious to read your stars than take your order. This can prove misleading. The familiarity of waitresses in some parts of the United States makes it easy to imagine that the world, his wife, and her teenage daughter are up for a one-night stand.★

Service matters. When 100,000 readers of the Zagat guides were asked what irritates them the most about restaurants, 74 percent cited service. Just 6 percent said bad food. So the people who greet you, take

---

★The famous intellectual Kevin Bacon once said, "Anybody can have sex when they're famous. I [had sex] a lot when I was not famous, and that was something I was very proud of back then. Being a waiter with no money, not a lot of drugs, just a mattress on the floor — and still being able to pull chicks. That's when you separate the men from the boys."

your coat, your order, and your tip are the ones who really count; they're the ones who dictate your opinion of the restaurant, whether you like it or not. "The ambience created by restaurant staff is vastly important," writes Michael Winner. "After all, you meet the staff before you meet the food. Sometimes a very long time indeed before you meet the food."

In theory, then, front-of-house staff are the midwives to a memorable dinner, but even when they're good, they rarely get any credit: one should not notice great service. It should, in effect, be invisible. "You should never have to ask for wine, bread, or water," says Silvano Giraldin, *éminence grise* at Le Gavroche. "You should never wonder when your food is going to arrive. You should never feel you are being rushed from one course to the next."

So we conclude that service is not what it was — for the privileged few. The restaurant world is a good deal more democratic than it used to be — doubtless a victory for the rest of us. Meanwhile, foodies chew on a moral dilemma: the sort of service we cherish is an emblem of a past that is largely discredited. I discovered this in the first-class dining compartment of the overnight train from Nairobi to Mombasa. This genteel refuge from anything so vulgar as the present is one of the most enduring emblems of colonialism. For a pittance, one is treated like the king of a small diamond-producing statelet. The silver service, monocled diners, and obsequious bows would all offend a socialist. But this was the epitome of good service, according to foodie law.

On this subject, it is difficult to argue with the gourmet pedants. I really don't like to be greeted by a lazy, resentful teenager. I want to be treated with some civility, and I don't think that's unconscionable. So, yes, it's good when the hostess remembers my name, the table is bathed in linen, the waiter has clean fingernails, and the chef is not on amphetamines. And, yes, I'd be happier if the whole world could eat like this. There's no excuse for bad service.

To be pampered in a European restaurant today, you go to one of those Michelin monsters, or some faded souvenir of Victorian Britain, where, as critic Matthew Fort puts it, "you can still relish the drama of the dining room — the flambéing, the filleting of fish with spoon and fork, the easy dismemberment of chicken or duck, the careful arrangement of elegant slivers on the plate, the ritual benediction of sauce."

I don't need that level of pampering. It doesn't make me feel any better about the species or myself. Somewhere between the faded souvenirs and the waitress who is really an actress, there is, however, a practicable solution. I'm not going there — we all know good service when we receive it, and this is not a staff manual — but I do propose to tackle a question that is seldom answered with any frankness: What is the *value* of good service?

One hundred years ago, tipping was widely regarded with disdain. A public campaign saw the "offensively un-American" practice outlawed in six states, with the tip being described — in a 1916 polemic, *The Itching Palm* — as the price "one American is willing to pay to induce another American to acknowledge inferiority." Today, staff in New York restaurants expect at least 18 percent ("double the tax"), and when you go out to a bar, you are "supposed to" tip a dollar on every drink. I resent this imposition, but the locals seem to love it, and waiters aren't about to stop them. As James Surowiecki put it in the *New Yorker* recently: "Diners like the power that the ability to tip gives them. Waiters like tipping because it gives them the chance to distinguish themselves from the crowd and to score an occasional windfall." Hence tipping, once viewed as an unpleasant reminder of the master–servant relationship, is somehow emblematic of capitalism.

I have a very intelligent friend called Noel who spent the 1990s working illegally in New York. I met him at a party in 1988, selling pot to students in the heart of bourgeois Dublin. He was caught, of course, and then he left. A nation mourns for grassy Noel, who should really be running a liberal democracy. Instead, he's scraping plates. What's more, he loves the job. When I asked him to explain why he has spent the last ten years as a busboy in a Midtown steakhouse of no great renown, he said, "It's partly the thrill of doing a new performance every night, partly the ritual of doing the same thing every night, and partly the fact that I can get shit-faced after work." *Bisexual* is too small a word for Noel, who has always been exotic. When he goes out to dinner, he thinks nothing of dropping a forty-buck tip on top of a hundred-dollar meal. Noel regards it a privilege to support people who live on the kindness of strangers. It is true, I suppose, that he has a vested interest in the kindness of strangers, being supported, as he is, by 129 million taxpayers. What's strange about Noel, however, is that his habits *are not so strange.* New Yorkers are legendary tippers.

Elsewhere, customs are quite different. In Japan, India, and Australia, tipping is optional or simply unnecessary. In Iceland, it is regarded as downright rude. At the end of your meal in France, Switzerland, Holland, and Belgium, you are given one check that includes all service and other charges. You are welcome to divest yourself of petty cash in homage to your cab driver, your waiter, or your kids. But you are not obliged to reach deep again, for all the little extras. Service puts pounds on a puny bill.

Earlier, I mentioned the White Hole, in which diners are duped into adding 25 percent of the bill as a tip. There is also the issue of where your money goes, prompting several others. Is the tip for your waiter alone? Will it be shared among all the staff, including the kitchen? Where does this largesse end? Will your gift be given to the owner's mistress, or the Chef de Rang's fifth child? Is tipping a sign of civilized society or proof that we live in the past?

The English journalist Bernard Levin had no time for the practice, on the basis that one should never tip an equal. "When you think of it," the journalist asked, "do you not feel that the entire business of tipping is not only distasteful, but shocking and almost evil?" Legally, we are not obliged to pay a service charge of any sort. When was the last time, however, that you saw someone refusing to reward a waiter? Levin believed that service should be included within the cost of dinner, so that customers are given a clear picture of how much they will have to pay, and, crucially, so that waiters will not be shafted. I think he was right.

It is time to reject the myth, an anomaly in a free-market economy, that tipping is essential so that waiters can have enough money to feed themselves. This self-serving guff answers itself. Try paying good wages to people who get none. Until that happens, the exchange between customer and waiter will always be fractious, one wishing for grace, the other demanding favor, while the owner of the restaurant plays us all for lackeys.

Eleven million people are now employed in American restaurants. Like anyone who has worked as a waiter, I know how easy it is to do the job with some enthusiasm and no great skill. That much was evident well before the end of my short career in silver service. Today, my sympathy is with the customer, and also with some small justice: I reserve the right to expose the waiter who acts like a seventeenth-century potentate, but the man who deserves yet more contempt is the one who refuses him a fair wage.

9

On Failing to Take Manhattan

1998–2000

HISTORY DOES NOT RECORD THE NAME OF THE WAG WHO stumbled on the following formula for success: sound Irish, dress British, think Yiddish. As a Dubliner with a public-school education and a Jewish father, I should thus be running a media empire. The figure who composed that axiom was rather more sanguine than wise, for he and I are equally anonymous. No matter. Kevin Kelly assumed that my background would open doors for him in New York, where everyone is sick of being told that the Irish built the place and the Jews now run it. "This is the big one," he kept repeating at a volume so low that I thought he might have lost his voice.

It is true that the Irish have some small sway. Bono is the only rock star with clout on Capitol Hill. Pierce Brosnan and Colin Farrell turned acclaim on the local stage into Stateside stardom. Then there's *Riverdance:* pretty young things in fetching skirts, proving once and for all that Irish dancing is *almost* sexy. Masochists can't get enough of this byword for cheese, whipping themselves into violent derangement about its cultural significance. One thinks, too, of Frank McCourt, who created a peculiarly American triumph in *Angela's Ashes.* (This last I take no pride in whatsoever. Joyce and Yeats lent men like McCourt a license to blabber for their country. Alan Parker has no such excuse. His film of the book was even worse, and he's not even Irish.)

So we travel well, embrace opportunity, and take offense when Americans assume that we are Brits. Maybe it's because we drink tea, like Sting's *Englishman in New York*. Maybe it's wishful thinking. When I arrived in the spring of 1998, the city was toying with all things Blighty, in the shape of Hugh Grant and two sisters called Plum and Lucy Sykes.★ Being Irish seemed no more fashionable than drowning puppies.

I was supposed to stay for two weeks, "researching the market." Once again, Kevin Kelly had other plans. I spent two years commuting between London and New York after Kelly made me the editor of *America's Elite 1,000*. Perhaps it was sage to ask a young Irishman who did not drive or wear a watch to chronicle the lifestyle of the great American billionaire. What a guy. What a job. When things got hairy — perfume launches are bad for the soul, and the sort of New Yorkers who hate perfume launches are not too keen on Irish dilettantes — we took out a map and picked up the phone.

"Hi. Is that the Dallas Polo Club? We're writing a book for billionaires. Will you host a reception for us?"

More often than not, the answer was yes. In Chicago, Los Angeles, and San Francisco, we were treated like tourists, if not the usual kind, for it must have seemed as if we really, really liked rich Americans. Shelby Hodge wrote the following account of a trip for the *Houston Chronicle*:

> Irishmen Kevin Kelly and Trevor White were the toast of the town this past week as they worked their way through some of

---

★I never met Grant, but often ran into the Sykes sisters. Plum was always icy, elegant, and "looking for Lucy," who was slightly plainer and more approachable. From the christening of yachts to Puff Daddy's parties in the Hamptons, the Sykes sisters were on hand to flatter the host and smile at well-dressed heirs. "They're twins!" cooed the *New York Times*. "They're thin. They're attractively employed, talented . . . Oh, and one other thing: they're English!"

the smartest drawing rooms and the finest restaurants in the city. They dined at Vallone's, lunched at Café Annie, bunked at the St. Regis and schmoozed with everyone from Lynn Wyatt to Dan and Pat Breen. And all the while they were making mental notes and taking names, picking the brains of all whom they encountered.

Kelly and White are working on *America's Elite 1,000*. This slick, beautifully executed book is a compendium of the good life in America. Need a real estate agent in Aspen, a landscape architect in Santa Monica, a custom framer of fine art in Atlanta or a private chef in Beverly Hills? Kelly and White have the answers.

This is a generous assessment of our work. The only mental notes I made were, "My, that restaurant/ring/ranch is big," and the names I took were simply to impress the next bunch of suckers who sat back, smiled, and said, "You boys are cute. Let's have lunch." However, it is true that I paid keen attention, and I did record the experience. Every night after work, I went to Starbucks to work on my screenplay about a young Irish hack whose function in life is to smile at wealthy old women from Texas. There, I became a laptop-lugging member of the Starbucks generation. It is also where I learned that the earnest plea of Starbucks chairman Howard Schultz ("The beverage is just a vehicle for crafting an experience . . . We're in the business of creating an experience around coffee and culture and the sense of community") was so much sanctimonious bullshit.

The screenplay lent my exploits a smidgeon of credibility. Not enough. So many Europeans — men like Wilder, Chaplin, Hitchcock — had been there before, with a lighter hand and a much better handle on what makes Gotham tick. Besides, it is hard to satirize something that does such a good job of satirizing itself. In the end, I resorted to facts. So the following speech by a character called Donald Trump is of no interest to people who love movies: "My name is Donald Trump, and I'm the largest real-estate developer in New York City. But I've been down. In 1991, I owed the banks $975 million. They were crawling all over me. The casinos were bleeding, Wall

Street went nuts, and the tabloids said I was yesterday's man. What do you think of me now?"

Five years later, Trump launched his own publication for the rich. *Trump World* is full of business and property tips for billionaires, as well as helpful advice on spending all that dough. He's still a mogul, his latest skyscraper is some ninety stories tall, but only if you skip eighteen floors along the way. "I call it truthful hyperbole," says The Donald, who has also starred in his own TV show. This is how he introduced himself: "My name is Donald Trump, and I'm the largest real-estate developer in New York. I own buildings all over the place, modeling agencies, the Miss Universe Contest, jetliners, golf courses, casinos, and private resorts."

A true survivor, Trump remains a wealthy man, even if he isn't quite as rich as he thinks. Titter if you must, but remember the corpses, too. In 1998, Kevin Kelly told me to interview a man called Ken Lay. Back then, there was a bullishness in the city that commentators, cab drivers, and my colleagues all compared to a year that no one could remember: 1929. If you had announced that five years from now the chairman of Enron will have died in disgrace, who would have believed you?

Historians will record that 1999 was the golden age of irrational exuberance. Wall Street was not a place but a state of grace. Even Henry Kravis, the model for Gordon Gekko, was by then reinvented as a merchant prince. The share price of Amazon.com had tripled in four months, Jean Georges was getting 4,000 calls a day, and *Vanity Fair* ran an article on the opening of Pastis, a pricey pastiche of an ordinary French bistro. Its location in the edgy Meatpacking District and a bizarre seating policy — no reservations, except for those with the secret number — ensured long lines. Chauffeurs vied with truck drivers for parking space, as some of the thinnest people in the northern hemisphere popped in for a glimpse of Ben Affleck and the guilty pleasure of a French onion soup.

I tried to avoid Pastis, though I do belong to an elite circle, of perhaps a million men. We all remember seeing Paris and Nicky

Hilton at parties in the summer of 1999. When you found yourself standing beside Paris at the bar, you didn't think, "Wow. Hot young heiress, porno princess." You thought, "Wow. That child is out very late. Again." Skimpily dressed, tall, and doe-eyed, in their early teens, the Hilton sisters were like the beginning of a movie that turns sour. We all know the story will end with some handsome frog, an addiction to charity balls, and three lousy kids, but I'm just telling you how it looked back then. They were pretty, but *it* wasn't pretty.

I also belong to the list of witnesses who saw John F. Kennedy Jr. rollerblading in Central Park (twice), and the even smaller number of people who have asked Gwyneth Paltrow to read their screenplay (once). At a lecture in Nolita, she scrawled an address on the back of my hand. Sweet. I went, handed in the script, and waited outside for twenty minutes, idly dreaming about dinner alone, just the two of us. I was tucking into sticky-toffee pudding and a glass of Barsac ("Would you like some more, darling?") when it struck me that there is a thin line between sticking around and stalking.

Reverie comes easily to the empty-headed. For several months, I got carried away with Kevin Kelly's plan. "We are making the world safe for luxury goods," I wrote to a colleague, "with all the ambition and frivolity that phrase suggests . . . Even Michelin, whose guides have dictated culinary trends in Europe for a hundred years, are reluctant to enter the American market. This is the first time that anyone has produced a social history of the good life in America at the dawn of the twenty-first century."

The plan was best appreciated after two martinis in the bar of the Carlyle Hotel, which Princess Diana called home in New York. One night, after the sort of session that Kevin Kelly called work, I stumbled out of the hotel and into a taxi. Arriving, tight, at the loft that I shared with two wise, lovable, older gay men, I was sent to bed with a copy of *The Diamond as Big as the Ritz:*

> "There are only diamonds in the whole world, diamonds and perhaps the shabby gift of disillusion. Well, I have that last and I

will make the usual nothing of it." He shivered. "Turn up your coat collar, little girl, the night's full of chill and you'll get pneumonia. His was a great sin who first invented consciousness. Let us lose it for a few hours."

Eating in New York can be a lot of fun. Reading restaurant reviews is a chore. The city that produced the Butcher of Broadway has a tradition of tough theater criticism, but its chefs are assessed by "twinks," as A. A. Gill recently said, "who want to let you know how aesthetically starched they are and what good taste they have. They think of themselves as men of letters. They want to be admired and liked. Wanting to be liked, or God forbid, admired, is agoraphobia to a critic."

While the city's magazines cover the restaurant scene with some imagination,★ its newspapers can seem forlorn, even apologetic. For example, when William Grimes was appointed as the chief critic of the *New York Times* in 1998, he quickly incurred the wrath of chefs by announcing his intention to expose charlatans. After much bellyaching, the verdicts appeared to get softer. On retiring from his post in 2004, the most powerful judge of cooking sent a love letter to the nation's chefs.

"A confluence of long-term and short-term trends conspired to make my tenure as restaurant critic an extended dream sequence of spectacular meals," wrote Grimes. "Young American chefs poured out of the culinary schools, eager to make their marks and firmly committed to the principles laid down nearly 30 years ago at Chez Panisse, where all meals were based on local produce and fresh ingredients."

His final words were: "The coming year looks auspicious. I just hope I can get reservations."

He will. Despite the appointment of Frank Bruni as Grimes's replacement, the situation remains disquieting. Top chefs cook for the

★The *New Yorker* and *New York* run short, droll, trenchant reviews, Jeffrey Steingarten's food column in *Vogue* is amusing and *GQ*'s Alan Richman — who calls honey "bee-puke" — has an outré charm. "I have been known," writes Richman, "to stand in front of my microwave, reheating coffee, wondering why it takes so long."

press in America, just as fashion designers toil for the handful of commentators who matter. The critical racket is less cultured in Britain, yet also more mature. Few wear silly disguises; a handful know what conscience means.

Haunted by objectivity, fancy dress, and (old-fashioned British) fair play, many critics cannot keep up with the curiosity and ambition of new cooking, nor the explosion in restaurant culture, and they have no time for the vulgar idea that critics are competing for readers' attention. The sort of people who ask for a glass of Chablis in Wendy's, they seem destined to give lectures on hygiene management.

To understand all this, a little context: in the second half of the twentieth century, neither of the clean-cut, wholesome cooks who first decided how Americans *should* dine were restaurant critics. With the stern brow and long skirt of an elementary-school teacher, Julia Child showed the nation how to cook. Then Alice Waters taught everyone about ingredients. The founder of Chez Panisse, Waters proved to a country raised on meatloaf that there is nothing wrong with fresh, local, seasonal food.

While Waters and Child were out in the field, Craig Claiborne was editing the food pages in the *New York Times*. When he was appointed in 1957, Claiborne banned press trips and free meals, on the basis that all food-related journalism should be treated as news, and thus subject to the same constraints. "When you remove the news," he told a successor, "you lose the vitality of a story, its ability to touch real lives, its slow and incremental way of reflecting the world. Before you know it, you have the God-awful pretension and solipsism that trivializes the entire subject and can only, in the end, compromise the reporter."

Those words convey something of Claiborne's moral authority, the emphasis that he put on anonymity — the reporter could only write an "objective" review if he was treated like any other customer — and the context in which Mimi Sheraton disguised herself as a lesbian poet in order to judge a meal. One might imagine that a sane person would be reluctant to disclose that information, but American critics recall such things with pride. In her memoir, *Eating My Words,* Sheraton boasts:

> Fueled by the romantic notion of undercover agents in disguise, I believe I was the first restaurant critic to collect a wardrobe of wigs. One was an auburn pageboy affair with straight bangs that I dubbed the Greenwich Village Lady Poet. A second, the Five Towns Macher, was done up as a silver-blonde bouffant cascading over one eye. The third was a long, loose, comb-down of black hair that partially obscured my face in the style of an anguished activist, perhaps more Mimi Montag than Susan Sontag.

While Mimi Sheraton was holding forth in auburn pageboy mode, Ruth Reichl was embarking on her own journey to culinary prominence. "She seems to have come to food not by passion, intellect, or pursuit," wrote Martha Stewart in a review of Reichl's second memoir, "but rather by escaping from a domineering, meddlesome, and selfish mother, who was such a bad cook that she regularly poisoned her guests."★

Ruth Reichl opened a restaurant in California in the 1970s, before drifting into food writing for the *Los Angeles Times* and, eventually, the *New York Times,* where she, too, became the proud owner of an outsize wig collection and several different aliases, each complete with childhood memories, personality, wardrobe, and Christian name.

By visiting a restaurant on two occasions, once in disguise and once as herself, Reichl exposed Le Cirque for having the wit to treat famous critics with care. What does this prove? The owner of Le Cirque is not an idiot, and the critic lives in fear of being identified. Perhaps she has good reason. That same owner, Sirio Maccioni, once

---

★Is Martha Stewart qualified to smirk at Reichl's origins? Born Martha Kostyra in New Jersey, she was the eldest of six children in a lower-middle-class Polish family. After stints as a model, student, and national icon, the relentless social climber turned her hand to stock trading, with grim consequences. America's homemaker did a six-month stretch in a prison that will henceforth be known as Camp Cupcake.

said to Reichl, "The King of Spain is waiting in the bar, but your table is ready." The line was supposed to illustrate the critic's power, but it also reveals something that she might, understandably, regret: a cosy relationship between judge and judged.

"New York critics still want to be part of the restaurant system," said A. A. Gill in 2004. "They want to be glad-handed and fêted as wise and astonishingly tasteful arbiters of gastronomy, and they want to get tables." Such intimacy is commonplace in America, where critics doth protest too much about objectivity. Donning a wig to review a restaurant may well illustrate a sincere concern for the facts. It also reveals a penchant for playing the prima donna.

There are several restaurants in Manhattan that deserve a little of the praise they receive. I lived around the corner from the Gramercy Tavern and spent thousands of dollars on one dish, the filet mignon with mashed potatoes and balsamic-onion relish. I also spent thousands of dollars on the baby chicken with roasted Brussels sprouts, chestnuts and pumpkin. Sitting in the bar — more informal than the main dining room — I savored the nightly performance at one of the most celebrated restaurants in America. At Gramercy Tavern, you get smart staff, the sense that someone has taken charge, consistently good food (allowing for occasional improvements), eclectic customers, a reasonable bill, and the sort of comfort one might expect in a wealthy old friend's house.

When you shake the owner Danny Meyer's hand and he's giving you that "Hi! Nice to *see* you!" patter, you get the impression that he is elsewhere. The patron glides around with easy languor, like a poor man's Jimmy Stewart. His smile is warm but hesitant. It's this tension in his personality that drives Meyer, and people like him, to create such extraordinary restaurants. You sense that he is constantly looking for ways to do things slightly more efficiently, or elegantly. Impressive. But, to be honest, that isn't the reason why I kept going back to Gramercy Tavern. Her name was Jodie, and she was the barmaid. Far too cynical to be that beautiful, Jodie belonged in film noir, the wise-talking sister, all heart or none. "Irish, you look tired," she would say, shaking a martini. "Still trying to make the world safe for rich people?"

Then there was Graydon Carter of *Vanity Fair*, lunching with Rupert Everett in Da Silvano (the Canadian editor of an American magazine, dining with a British film star, in an Italian restaurant in New York). Kevin Kelly wanted to meet Carter, so I marched up to the table and demanded to know if the editor had received his preview copy of *America's Elite 1,000*. "Sure, I got it. So what?" snapped Carter, with the insouciance of all great hacks. Recoiling, I slipped into a sycophantic rant about the editor's finely coiffed locks. But it was too late. Carter wanted rid of the pest.

"What are you, a *hairdresser?*"

In his memoir, *How to Lose Friends and Alienate People*, the English journalist Toby Young recalls his stint as a writer at *Vanity Fair*, which came to an end after a drunken dispute about a restaurant bill. In a memorable vignette, Graydon Carter reminds his new charge that New York is not as easy to crack as the young and the foolish imagine:

> You think you've arrived, doncha? I hate to break it to you but you're only in the first room. It's not nothing — don't get me wrong — but it's not that great either. Believe me, there are plenty of people in this town who got to the first room and then didn't get any further. After a year or so, maybe longer, you'll discover a secret doorway at the back of the first room that leads to the second room. In time, if you're lucky, you'll discover a doorway in the back of the second room that leads to the third. There are seven rooms in total and you're in the first. Doncha forget it.

The first time I met Toby Young was in the summer of 1994, when I shared the living-room floor of an apartment off Bowery on the Lower East Side. Three lads had actual bedrooms for weekend seduction, but I didn't mind. Squalor was a small price to pay for the glamour of being in Gotham with a gang of pals from Dublin. I had just spent a year in Bermuda and had all the pluck of an Irish priest banging on the door of the local whore. Young was newly arrived at *Vanity Fair* after the un-happy demise of his own magazine. "High culture for low brows," the *Modern Review* made me imagine that it might be possible to start my own little rag one day.

People said Young was a bit of a crank, which further impressed me. On the night I met him, we were kicked out of the Bowery Bar after he threw himself at a bouncer, the lazy provocation of the truly shit-faced. It was the hippest bar in the city at the time, largely because of one customer. Why did Leonardo DiCaprio have to witness my flight from door to curb? Picking myself up, I remember being embar-rassed and very, very conscious that one day I would write about the gibbering, stuttering, shouting fool who lay before me.

Five years later, I asked Young to write a story for the second edi-tion of *America's Elite 1,000*. As an Englishman in New York, he was perfectly placed to document the influence of Europeans in America. "Years ago," I wrote in an e-mail, "nouveau riche Americans would travel to Savile Row to have their suits made by sniffy English tailors. The same English tailors have now gone west. Let's talk to them."

Young didn't, of course. Instead, he delivered a savage rant about the pretense and stupidity of Europeans who think they can crack New York:

> When I first moved to New York, I thought society hostesses would be falling over themselves to invite me to parties and the richest men in America would be queuing up to introduce me to their daughters. Five years later, I now know that being European is an enormous handicap. As far as most New Yorkers are con-cerned, you're just another freeloading parasite, out to fleece the locals for whatever you can get.
>
> The days when a European accent, a decent education and a name which sounded like an entrée at Da Silvano were all you needed to get laid in New York are far behind us, I'm afraid. Nowadays, we're just another ethnic group battling for our slice of the American pie, no different from the Pakistanis. It won't be long before we're driving New York cabs.

Showing this diatribe to my patron was the low point of my career. I still remember the look of disgust on Kevin Kelly's face. He couldn't even bring himself to finish reading, and I felt rotten for sharing the article. It was like telling Steven Spielberg that Israel has decided to refuse him a visa.

One afternoon, I rang Young's apartment to invite him to lunch with some advertisers. I figured some cheek might lend the event a little fizz. A woman who sounded like Marilyn Monroe answered the phone. "Toby's not in," she whispered, "but I can help you."

The following day, Sophie Dahl joined ten clients and me for lunch in Jean Georges. The model behaved like someone who had spent her life in the company of tedious strangers. Flattering, prying, laughing, and conspiring, she was the star of the day, and a secret star at that. Unknown in America, where she had just arrived and had yet to garner so much as a mention in the columns of "Page Six," Dahl reveled in brief anonymity. At the end of the meal, I asked if she needed a ride downtown. We fell into a taxi, laughing about the earnestness of a restaurant that serves a dozen different types of water. I announced that I had plans, big plans, but Sophie's no fool, so I told her the truth. My career was a Faustian pact.

"Oh yeah?" she replied.

"Yes," I said. "I spend my life in restaurants I like, in the company of people I don't."

I was pleased with that miserable line, and with myself, for orchestrating such a result. She sighed, then smiled, in the manner of a woman who knows that her eyes can finish a sentence. Sophie Dahl had just gone to lunch with a lot of strangers, and was now indulging my delusion.

We launched *America's Elite 1,000* in New York's most famous restaurant. With all its faux splendor, Le Cirque — then housed in the landmark Villard Houses — was the perfect venue for such a preposterous celebration. It was all yellow and red, like a McDonald's for millionaires. I knew the restaurant well, having interviewed the owner, Sirio Maccioni, for *Food and Wine* the year before. We put him on the cover — of an Irish magazine — so that Kevin Kelly could be certain of a table whenever he was in New York.

In public, Maccioni was one of the last great hosts, a man so charismatic that women would gasp and men would fawn, all aflutter at the thought of an audience with the grand old gentleman of Europe. He presided over a restaurant in which celebrities bagged the best tables, and he knew long before anyone else that free courses — more starters, some risotto, a chocolate surprise — are the way to charm both critics and tycoons. In private, however, Maccioni was the most self-effacing man I have ever met. His wife was the cook in the family. He didn't give a fig for formality, readily admitted his contempt for the boardroom battles that were daily played out in his restaurant, and liked nothing better than some shared rudeness, a glass of Barolo, and a little kitchen gossip. Perhaps it was his very informality — disarming, convivial — that drove thousands of otherwise normal people to get so uptight in his company.

Five hundred of the usual suspects piled into Le Cirque for a glass of free Champagne. They also came, of course, to inspect *America's Elite 1,000*. They craned their necks and crinkled their brows, pretending to take it seriously. After gazing at the columns of names in the book, of decorators, architects, hotels, galleries, and restaurants, some of the grandees sniggered. A group of women from out of town had genuine compliments to offer the publisher and his blushing lackey. As one of them left with a copy tucked under her arms, I imagined her putting it on a coffee table, where it would stay for years, and I saw her grandchildren, many decades later, flicking through the book in silent alarm.

What was she like, this woman who would put our book on her coffee table? What sort of people like to read lists of powerful, good-looking strangers? Like most arrivistes, they are neither powerful nor good looking. I picture them squeezed onto the worst table in the best new restaurants, asking if the chef is free for a moment. I have seen them in the Hamptons, falling out of Jet East, and I have seen them three days later, hogging the view at La Goulue. The sort of American who wants to read books about luxury goods is rich enough to admire Europe, but not stylish enough to avoid being defined by his clothes, his car, and his watch. To the empty mind, appearance matters.

At the end of the night, I interrupted Kevin Kelly in the middle of his dinner with Ivana Trump. "Well done," I said, with one last smile. And then I went out to play pool. Alone.

The book made a modest impression in the media, and for once I was happy that American foodies think it cruel to bite. An expensive PR company got us into a couple of the gossip columns. "Lovingly put together by Trevor White," wrote Liz Smith, "*America's Elite 1,000* will be a coffee-table must, more entertaining for who and what it leaves out than for who and what is included." Naturally, Ms. Smith was among the fêted. CNN ran a spot, which allowed Kevin Kelly to communicate his vision of the world to the viewers of its business channel at three o'clock in the morning. I remember being annoyed that the interview was broadcast in the middle of the night. Looking back, the timing could not have been more appropriate. The nation wanted *Angels in America*. We gave them the bastard love child of *Dynasty* and *Dallas*.

Two months after the launch of *America's Elite 1,000*, Kurt Andersen's *Turn of the Century* was published to critical acclaim. The novel's heroine, Lizzie, was born in the world that Kevin Kelly tried to conquer. If he had succeeded, perhaps he would share her view of the world: "[Lizzie had] begun to see all the Bel Air and Park Avenue *wanting* as a perverse romanticism, vanity, and self-advancement pursued so monomaniacally that they turn inside out and become a kind of naivety, the naivety of children." In that sentence, Andersen captures the true spirit of *America's Elite 1,000*. It wasn't until I read his novel that I realized what the book I had edited was all about.

Our billionaire's phone book was a waste of money. I am not, however, so ungrateful as to call it a waste of time. Kevin Kelly hired me to come along for the ride, and for the most part it was quite exhilarating. Kelly, who could turn on the blarney like no one I have ever seen, taught me all about publishing, and his love of the business was contagious.

I never did finish that screenplay, and my boss never found a diamond as big as the Ritz. He blamed the failure of his project on 9/11, but the book was a disaster well before the Twin Towers fell. Even at the height of a spectacular boom, elitism got the cold shoulder. Our abject failure suggests that Americans have better taste than Europeans imagine. That sentiment will not play well in Europe, but then, we have so much to learn about, and from, America.

In Ireland, you're no one unless you hate George Bush. When friends carp about his misdeeds, I don't pretend that he is a statesman. I do remind them, however, that Bush has much to protect. The inability to distinguish between American foreign policy and American people points to a fault in the European mind that is more sinister than anything you will find in The Moronic Inferno.

I did not take Manhattan. I didn't even get to the first room. However, I saw enough of America to realize that it doesn't really matter where you come from. Being Irish or Jewish means very little unless you have something to offer. Sophie Dahl; Toby Young; Sirio Maccioni; Graydon Carter: all privileged, no doubt, but their stories illustrate something about the United States that is rarely understood by people who have not lived there. In the adopted home of Charlie Chaplin, Billy Wilder, and Alfred Hitchcock, one really believes that an empty stomach and a good idea will find reward.

That's why I should have starved.

THE FOOD CRITIC ORDERS DINNER

"I'll have the inevitable quiche Lorraine with an elegantly airy custard filling but a disappointingly soggy pastry, the rather bland and textureless gazpacho, and the slightly-dry-from-overcooking calves' liver lightly garnished with tasteless, oily onions."

10

"Your Table Is Ready"

The Four Sweetest Words

Surely the restaurant is one of civilisation's great achievements. Since it was not there, the French had to invent it, long before the Revolution — a restaurant was a cauldron of restorative stew into which patrons for a few sous plunged their bowls and helped themselves — and very soon it caught on elsewhere. As how would it not, the idea being so simple and so sweet. That one may, for a relatively small out-lay of cash, walk freely into someone else's dining room and be greeted by an affable, clean and well-dressed person who will smilingly show you to your table, offer you a drink, take diligent note of what you would like to eat and then go and fetch it for you, all the while pretending to be your friend, is a remarkable freedom and a rich pleasure, unique in this vale of tears.

— John Banville, *The Dubliner* magazine

AMONG THE MANY REASONS WHY A GOURMET LOVES DINING OUT is the fact that it demands some public expression of taste. There is something richly satisfying about that, but food has little enough to do with it. The secondary decisions — how we arrive, where we sit, how much patience we muster, the tone in which we order, what subjects are deemed suitable for conversation — reveal more about us than what we choose to consume.

Cooks like dining out; students of psychology or history are just as likely to savor the experience. For instance, one of the pleasures of eating in a formal restaurant is the opportunity it affords to fake involvement in something of great significance. When we raise a menu — as a dowager might once have raised a fan — and share a hushed confidence with someone who sits less than two feet away, we suddenly become participants in a ritual that is old and possibly rather menacing. With the obvious exception of sex in a crowded railway station, there may be no greater public pleasure.

In his book *Feast,* Sir Roy Strong charts the social history of dinner, "a way of sustaining and reiterating the social order." From the extravagant spectacles of Ancient Rome through the culinary Dark Ages, when the Catholic Church became the only arbiter of table etiquette, and on then to the medieval period, with its trestle tables laden with flagons of wine, Strong explores the history of the world through man's behavior in the dining room. By the time we get to the Renaissance, the emergence of more private dining becomes an expression of social status, and there is a renewed emphasis on classical values: "a submission to appetite without guilt, and a rejection of the pious eating dominated by liturgy."

It is arguable that private dining paved the way for the revolutions of the nineteenth century, for reasons that now seem prosaic: confidential discussion is invariably more candid, even conspiratorial, and a round table favors no one, thus encouraging all. The theory is impossible to prove, which explains why the erudite Strong does not indulge it for long. In his conclusion, however, he does claim that a shared meal "usually involves the manipulation of one group by another for sociopolitical aims." If this seems a bit cynical, think of the dinner party, that Victorian invention in which suburban archetypes try to outdo each other. Or have lunch in a very good restaurant.

That unlovely term "power lunch" was first used to describe the rush of titans to New York's Four Seasons, the original billionaire's café (nothing to do with the excellent hotel group of the same name). Twelve clients have daily reservations in the Four Seasons, where deal-makers are not distracted by elaborate tableside service, and lunch rarely lasts more than ninety minutes. This is the dining room in which Marla Maples was served with a subpoena on behalf of Ivana Trump, and where an animal rights activist dropped a dead raccoon on Anna Wintour's table, shouting, "Anna wears fur hats!"

One rarely sees a headline made at lunch, though it happens all the time. In politics, media, advertising, and show business, deals are brokered in the regal surroundings of formal restaurants, and table-hopping is truly practiced as an art form. This is not just serendipity; one has to admire the ingenuity of a person who uses a dining room as an office. At places like Le Cinq in Paris and the Ivy in Los Angeles, billions of dollars change hands every year, between the fall and rise of a napkin. As A. A. Gill said of The Ivy, "To the terminally cynical, it might look like a lot of luvvies air-kissing, but it's the laboratory that produces so much of the stuff you call culture."

Some people are too busy scoffing at the rituals to appreciate their significance; others think that dining out is not for amateurs. One of those positions is self-defeating, the other is imbecilic. This is not about snobbery, inverted or otherwise. It really does pay to learn the rules.

First, you need a reservation.

For a certain sort of person — acquisitive, hungry, slave to fashion — the sweetest words in the English language are "Your table is ready." In Whites on the Green, I discovered that people are happy to lie or threaten a stranger just to hear that declaration. The *New York Times* has tackled this sensitive subject in order to advance our knowledge of the human condition. In 1998, the paper decided to expose the crimes that customers commit in order to secure a seat at Manhattan's top tables. As it was the paper of record, the story was presented with mouth agape. Diners were divided into seven different categories, like so many naughty schoolchildren:

1. **Celebrity Impersonators.** The staff doesn't even know if the pseudo Harrison Ford is even called Harrison Ford, because he always pays in cash.

2. **Outright Thieves.** Diner crawls to the front of the line, has a peep of the reservation book, and literally steals someone else's table.

3. **Owner's Best Pals.** Sirio Maccioni of Le Cirque: "People often tell me that they are a dear friend of the owner, Sergio."

4. **Name-Droppers.** Append the words *princess, duke,* or *lord* to your name when booking. Or call on your own behalf, claiming to be your secretary.

5. **Epic Bards.** "I told one walk-in that he'd have to wait an hour for a table. He said, 'I can't wait that long.' I asked, 'Why?' He said, 'I only have six months to live, and every moment is precious to me.' How could you not give that guy a table?"

6. **Bribers.** They offer money in hilariously contrived ways, secreting bills between fingers and in palms, "as if they'd seen it done in a bad movie."

7. **Great Intimidators.** "Do you know who I am?" is so passé. Mouth slowly: "If you don't give me a table at eight o'clock tomorrow, I will blow this restaurant up tonight."

The article ended with a stern reminder that Parisians are much worse than New Yorkers. According to the *New York Times,* the French have "raised celebrity impersonation to an art." Do I detect the beating heart of that great newspaper? One suspects that New Yorkers would give Parisians a run for their money in that department.

Here are seven legal, moral, and perfectly legitimate ways to get a reservation at short notice in a good restaurant:

1. **Walk in at 7:30 p.m.** Small parties often fail to show up for the first sitting, and you might just get lucky.

2. **Take a late reservation.** If you can be seated before 11 p.m. and the restaurant is really as hot as they say it is, you will have fun.

3. **Make friends with the staff or the owner.** This may seem slightly venal, but it's better than lying about it.

4. **Offer to sit at the bar.** In many formal restaurants, eating at the bar feels like a privilege, and if you're alone you may just meet good company.

5. **Go on Monday.** Often the quietest night of the week. In Manhattan, however, the pattern is reversed, as vaguely important people leave town at the weekend.

6. **Try to book by fax.** It's hard to turn down a smart typed letter of inquiry.

7. **Arrive with someone who makes mouths drool.** Again, hard to turn down.

If you really want to, you can get into virtually any restaurant, as long as you are dressed in clothes that do not advertise your favorite sports team. The trick is to ask the maître d' with a warm smile, "Would you try to find us a table if we sat at the bar?" Courtesy is far more impressive than bluster.

"I always do my best to get people a table," Jesus Adorno-S., the Bolivian maître d' at Le Caprice in London, once told a newspaper. "But sometimes it's impossible. Not long ago, some people came in who didn't have a reservation. I apologized and explained that we were full — and so one of them threatened to beat me up. So I turned to him and said very politely, 'But Sir, if you do that I won't be able to get you a table at all.'"

Getting the best table is another matter. Every Jewish mother frets about this at some point. There is no substitute for experience. So the first time you go to a restaurant, ask the waiter to tell you the number of the table at which you would rather be sitting. When he does so, you can either write the number down, or smile, lower your voice and mention your incurable disease. All restaurants have a Siberia; debutantes, drunks, and jocks find it before everyone else.

It is worth noting that in Manhattan, the best table is often beside the front door — moguls like a draught, it seems — while in Paris the most secluded alcove is traditionally given to regulars, but only if it affords a view of proceedings. In Spain, you won't see any action before 10 p.m., while the English like to sit down for dinner between 8 and 8:30 p.m.* In certain parts of the United States, the locals are often in bed by then, while New Yorkers are thinking about dessert — unless they are particularly rich or famous, in which case they're crossing Central Park, hungry. To the seasoned table watcher, these things matter.

In bigger cities, many restaurants impose two sittings. The rule here is to avoid the earlier one, unless (a) you have jet lag, or (b) the *prix-fixe* menu offers good value. If you are sitting down at six thirty or seven o'clock, make sure that you have somewhere improbably glamorous to go to when you are ejected at four minutes to nine.

Travelers should note that hotel porters are paid to send business to certain restaurants. When they offer to help you with your dinner reservations, it is not because they know you are a renowned gourmet, in town for a couple of days to find the best chef. It is because they will receive a small sum from the manager of your dinner venue. You may not enjoy it. Any restaurant that courts business so aggressively is rarely overburdened by customers. Try not to find out why.

---

*In 1962, Egon Ronay, owner of the eponymous guides, turned up late for dinner at the Manor House in Moretonhampstead, Devon. His opinion of the hotel now reads like social history. It also reveals the gulf between the genteel criticism of the past and the rabid dogs of dinner. This is the harshest report in Egon Ronay's guide that year:

The head waiter refused to serve me with hot dinner at about 9 p.m. here at the height of the season, in spite of my firm references to their four AA stars. So I am including it only because of the good cooking and well-known wine lists I have experienced in so many other British Railways-owned hotels. Well, not only because of that. This palatial, luxury hotel seemed so well kept, to have so much comfort, and is so magnificently situated, that you would be the loser for missing it even if you have to get there at puritanic hours.

Dining out is more satisfying than the uninitiated imagine, and the rituals of dinner are not difficult to master. To close this chapter, here are ten commandments to consider before you venture out on that date with the total stranger who stands between you and the realization of your disgusting sexual fantasies.

1. **Don't go to restaurants that offer you a table at half past anything.** If the owners are watching the clock that closely, they don't know the meaning of hospitality.

2. **If you want good food, don't worry about the glorious waterfront view.** Or, as Andy Rooney put it, in a slightly different context: "Never trust the food in a restaurant on top of the tallest building in town that spends a lot of time folding napkins."

3. **If you want a good table for two, book for three.** Rather impudent, but worth remembering for special occasions.

4. **If you are shown to a bad table, request a better one.** The definition of bad depends on whether you are an exhibitionist. Some diners love sitting in full view of a crowded room, while others dislike the stage. No one likes to sit beside the toilet.

5. **Go to lots of family-owned restaurants.** There is some satisfaction in knowing that your money is supporting a clan, and not a corporation.

6. **Request a corner table.** Particularly if you are on a date. Sitting at a right angle is more flattering than facing each other.

7. **Ask "What is the best thing on the menu?"** Any good waiter will have a reasonable answer at the ready. If the food is half as good as he says it is, you'll be lucky.

8. **If you aren't completely happy with your meal, send it back — quickly.** It is unwise, and possibly dangerous, to describe the food on a nearly empty plate as inedible.

9. **When a man is served before a woman, that means you're welcome to leave before paying.** If you regard chivalry as ancient gibberish, you don't deserve to eat well.

10. **Avoid restaurants where people say, "Hi, my name is Hilary. I'm from Perth and I'll be your server tonight."** Unless you're a man, alone, and her name is Peach, from Georgia.

11

The Lamppost and the Dog

Writing about the Racket

WITH OUR SCHEME TO CONQUER HIGH SOCIETY, KEVIN KELLY and I were soon exposed as interlopers. I did eat well in New York, and greater crimes have been committed in search of good sashimi, but the targets of our tacky offensive merely thought us gauche, and this soon became embarrassing.

In September 2000, I decided to call it quits on the good-life racket. I had a dream for a magazine, and while Manhattan was an inspiration — I had been in the city when bold new glossies like *Talk* and *George* were launched; it was during that moment when magazines felt important — the plan had to be executed elsewhere. Hanging up my toothpick, I came home, clutching two pieces of paper. One of them was from an anonymous article in the *Sunday Times:*

> There is trouble ahead in the media's easy relationship with the middle classes. The future will be brash, even tasteless, and you will pay for every minute of it. Newspapers and magazines will become ever more attractive as a refuge for people in search of civilised values.

The second was a poem, written by Louis MacNeice in the 1950s. Called *Dublin,* it describes a place that could not be ignored:

> *She holds my mind with her seedy elegance,*
> *With her gentle veils of rain*
> *And all her ghosts that walk*
> *And all that hide behind*
> *Her Georgian facades —*
> *The catcalls and the pain,*
> *The glamour of her squalor,*
> *The bravado of her talk.*

Like an aging tart in a brand-new dress, the city had changed. It was more fashionable than ever before (the *Rough Guide* calls it "Ibiza in the rain"), and there was plenty of money around. "Thoreau would enjoy this town," I noted in an article for *Madison* magazine, "where the mass of men look like lottery winners." But there was angry talk, too, about a corrupt establishment, a church on the ropes, and the erosion of anything that might be called Irish. All perfect subjects for the city magazines that flourish in New York. There were none in Dublin.

We launched *The Dubliner* in January 2001. The party was held in City Hall, which had just reopened after a $10 million refurbishment. Sophie Dahl met several hundred strangers, and much champagne was drunk. Newspaper cones full of fish and chips were ferried down from a local chipper. California rolls kept the foodies from grumbling.

Our restaurant reviews soon spawned reviews of their own: they were "priceless, and slightly horrifying — particularly for chefs," or "a fantastically bitchy lash at the sacred cows of the Dublin restaurant scene." Those reviews — short, unashamedly candid — quickly became the most popular part of the magazine. Within a week, we badly needed a good lawyer.

On one level, it is understandable that restaurateurs are sensitive to criticism. Owning a restaurant is a difficult job. Only an exhibitionist or a masochist would want some pimpled stranger to judge, in public, a dream one had — a dream, remember, that may well result in the loss of one's car, one's house, and one's marriage. And, like all dreams, there is something unlikely, if not impossible, about the aspiration. This is Tim Zagat's advice for would-be restaurateurs:

> First you need to be a real estate expert to get a good location. You need to be a good designer to have a place that's comfortable to sit in, a good buyer to get the right produce at the right time, a good PR person, a good manager of people, a good server, a good cook, and you must be willing to work long days. On top of that, restaurants have the biggest failure rates among businesses in the country.

Spare a thought, too, for the chap in the kitchen. When you meet a chef who says that everyone loves his food, you know he's a pathological liar. The only things that chefs get all the time are grief, piles and piles of grief. No wonder they hate the genial hack. With apologies to John Osborne, asking a chef what he thinks about critics is like asking a lamppost what it thinks about dogs.

In America, critics are leading members of the culinary establishment. In Britain, chefs and the press largely keep a cool distance. They meet in the courts, or bed (few meet in restaurants; it's just too suspicious). Our little world is quite that incestuous, full of loathing and secret alliances. The sex is a function of human nature and/or alcohol. Animosity reflects the butt-clenching paranoia of chefs, and the fact that a critic's stock in trade, opinion, is a grubby, uncomfortable device, not something that saves lives like medicine or poetry, nor a thing to mend a broken heart.

The first obligation of a critic is to tell the truth, insofar as that is ever obtainable. The second obligation is to serve the reader. Chef's vanity is some way down the line. This news is not well received. Chefs rarely understand the difference between journalism and public relations, and if they do, they think of reviews in the same way that most of us regard cosmetic surgery: it could boost your ego, but might just ruin your life. Probably not worth risking. So they live in perpetual fear of the knife. As a critic, you are the guy with the knife. On the face of it (sorry), this seems quite absurd. In real life, as everyone knows, it is the chef who wields a blade. But the restaurant world is *not* real life.

In Dublin, most chefs could not be bothered to acknowledge a good review. Perhaps this is due to some fear that consorting with the enemy is unwise, even after a public blow job. The response to bad reviews is more interesting. Older cooks, the sort of people who know that success and failure really are impostors, are inclined to let the whole matter rest, while a few have even thanked me for exposing some woe (that salty chowder, the bitch at reception). Younger chefs are more inclined to seek vengeance. The most common response to a bad review is a hastily drafted letter, full of veiled threats, false magnanimity — "I know you are just doing a job, but . . ." — and an over-reliance on one word: lawyer. Chefs have stopped me in the street to casually announce that I have ruined their lives, which is nice. Still more have sought revenge. I have variously been assailed, poisoned, asked to leave a restaurant, and physically assaulted with a goddamn ladle.

This is not a class issue. People who own chip shops are no more likely to murder hacks; in fact, men who run classy joints are touchier than other restaurateurs. When Sir Terence Conran got a bad review, he sent a letter to his staff, responding to the "abusive and libellous" attack on his business. "Sadly," wrote Conran, "food critics have been encouraged to write in an emotional, amusing and personal way rather than offering readers well-considered and educated information. I doubt they fully understand the distress they cause to hard-working and dedicated people who run restaurants."

Conran is right to suggest that journalists mold truth to serve good prose.★ Many critics have far more style than substance, and it is true that some are insensitive, just as quite a few are bloody idiots.

★In a 1998 review of Sartoria, Craig Brown said Terence Conran was "nothing if not a designer, which is really just an old-fashioned name for control freak, itself a new-fangled way of saying bossyboots."

Fundamentally, however, the mogul's plea for "well-considered and educated information," i.e., good reviews, seems a bit rich. Critics enjoy the same freedom of speech that allows Conran to bite back. If a restaurant is consistently ripping off all of its customers, for example, it feels like a public service to say as much. Like imposing two sittings for dinner, or reserving the right to throw customers out, mouthing off in public is part of life in a democracy. Indeed, a tradition of robust criticism is one of the things that distinguishes a liberal democracy from a dictatorship. This fact lends the activity a little tenability; not much, but enough to expose a crank.

When said crank starts to grumble, it helps to have some muttered response to mind, if not always ready to mouth.

"The head chef was not on duty."

Tough. Whether a punter goes to a restaurant once or half a dozen times is irrelevant. You paid for a service, and you deserve value every time. As a representative of the public, critics are entitled to have the same expectations. Restaurant owners: if the chef is off, and that is such a problem, why not halve your prices for the night?

"You didn't write anything about the food."

Provide a reason to remember your work. We soon forget most restaurants. Words fail unmemorable food.

"Call yourself a critic? You're a fraud, a liar, and an alcoholic."

Nobody likes to face such a charge. It is like asking the bishop why he has a wife, sleeps with altar boys, and worships the devil. Unfair, and indefensible. Remember, the best revenge is that not taken. Or sue the bastard.

A related issue — it emerged, for me, in the west of Ireland — also deserves some scrutiny. Is objectivity possible, or even desirable? Can one provide an impartial account that is both faithful to one's experiences and fair to the restaurant? There are two theories. In the first, that intrepid gourmet who reviews a restaurant on the basis of five meals in five disguises is the one true critic. It sounds almost kinky:

cross-dressing up to take chefs down; a different costume every night; the public confession of a private fantasy.★

The other theory on objectivity is more logical, less exotic. Anonymity is a nonsense. The chef can't change the decor or the menu just because he knows that a critic is in the house; all he can do is his best. If it's not good enough, he deserves to be exposed. When you offer money for food, you enter into a social contract, with all the obligations that term implies. You are expected to behave with due decorum, observing both the customs of the day and the rules of the house. As for your host, he has obligations, among them, say, is the need to leave you satisfied, without insulting your wife or stealing your wallet.

In a restaurant, you are a customer, paying for a service. This fact will not ensure that you get the best table or a last-minute reservation on Christmas Eve. But it does entitle you to judge your experience, and to share it with anyone who wants to listen. Whether you sample a menu once or half a dozen times is irrelevant. You are paying for a service, and as such you are entitled to judge it. What do you do if your car breaks down on the day you buy it? You holler and roar until someone does something about it, and to hell with objectivity. In a restaurant, as a punter with a pen and an appetite, you can either do that yourself, or read about the genius who gave you gastroenteritis.

Professional restaurant critics regard themselves with awe for proving the existence of free lunch, as if the achievement were comparable to putting a Frenchman on Mars or shouting down Gordon Ramsay.

★Sometimes the mask slips. Writing in the *New York Times* about the closure of the legendary Lutèce in 2004, Ruth Reichl conceded: "It's true that the restaurant had four stars during the last years of André Soltner's reign, but it was a sentimental rating: nobody (including me) wanted to take anything away from him." In that tender valediction, Reichl does not hesitate to expose the bankruptcy of her own rating system. For someone so obsessed with her own detachment, the confession seems unusual, but it is, at least, humane.

My own career is emblematic: typical of a generation that reads more menus than recipes, I suggest how easy it is to become a critic. In fact, in an era of personal and participatory media, when journalism resembles not a sermon but a conversation, it is not even necessary to become a quote-unquote professional.

The New Restaurant Critics

Until the 1980s, the only people who offered an opinion on tea in public were food writers, gourmets, cricket captains, and the bridegroom, albeit briefly. The market has traditionally been dominated by the gourmet — French or American, and the subject of quite enough attention. For the first time in history, the bookish cooks of earnest broadsheets now have competition. Many critics belong to one or more of the following categories:

The Gourmand is the sort of person who steals the menu from a very good restaurant, and returns to it in moments of quiet gloom. Food means a lot to him, but not so much that he feels compelled to blanch and steam and boil each night. He prides himself on eating well, as he scans the menu of a reputable Chinese takeout.

The Celebrity is drafted in to provoke and prance for the benefit of his nubile companion. He thinks writing 600 words about a meal each week is "hard work." Likes the words "me" (viz. "That's the thing about me") and "historic."

The English Impatient shocks readers, and rarely flatters restaurateurs. When a new place opens, he rushes like judge and jury — with all the other dogs of dinner — as if to the scene of a poisoning. The fact that he clears his plate with unusual celerity does not console the mature chef.

The Roué is a man with a violet proboscis. When he dies, an obituary will record this fact with recourse to the standard euphemism: "There never was a finer judge of claret." Scientists debate the difference between The Gourmet and The Roué. Some believe there is none.

⋆   ⋆   ⋆

The easiest way to broadcast an opinion about the success or failure of a meal is on the Web. Most towns have an online forum for precisely this purpose, and many companies have in-house restaurant guides that represent the collective opinions of staff members. A friend of mine works in a large law firm that has a popular online database of reviews. It is housed on a secure server, but as my friend is a lawyer, she thought nothing of giving me the password to prove a point.

"Check it out," she wrote in an e-mail. "And note the time most reviews are posted. Just before lunch! People paid to defend reputations routinely spend the morning defaming their own clients!"

It is not often that one sees lawyers in such a warm, fuzzy light. Here were opinions expressed in elegant, forceful language. Treacherous assaults on laughably overpriced menus. Shame such opinions are seldom expressed in print, thanks to those same lawyers. Libel is the scourge of all critics, and, with the exception of people who run the very largest and the very smallest publications, editors are reluctant to indulge a loudmouth. Hence many of the most forthright and amusing reflections on restaurant culture are now found on the Web, where freedom of speech means glib expression and more, much more, than merely a glib expression.

Are the media moguls worried? Does the emergence of the Internet spell doom for Michael Winner? It is notable that some British newspapers and many newspaper Web sites now encourage readers to share their views in print, alongside the opinions of self-styled professionals. How long will this last? How long, indeed, will it be before newspapers themselves migrate to the Web for good?

The barbarians are not at the gate. They are in the kitchen, raiding the fridge.

Tim Zagat's advice to restaurateurs was good, but he was wrong about one thing. There is a business with a higher failure rate than restaurants. I know, because I left a well-paid job, crossed an ocean, and remortgaged my home in order to enter that business.

In its first nine months, *The Dubliner* lost three hundred thousand dollars. After that, I put on thirty pounds, worked Christmas Day, and really started to enjoy reviewing restaurants. When I sat down with my accountant at the end of that first year, the plan was to stay alive, which we all plan to do and invariably fail. Could I turn the rag around? Or would it go the way of *Talk* and *George*?

Dublin is not New York, but the city is big enough, certainly, to swallow me whole. This much I learned in year two.

Part Two

12

Silly Season in the Wilderness

Food, Politics, and Morgan Spurlock

I N THE SUMMER OF 2004, SOMETHING HAPPENED THAT LEFT ME, AND the book you are reading, with a case to answer. Each morning at *The Dubliner* felt like the start of some new battle, and elsewhere, too, no peace. Some time earlier, a journalist at the *Irish Times* had made a basic error in reading the accounts of *The Dubliner*, undermining what confidence there was in the market. My relationship with the *Irish Times* improved, briefly, when I was hired as its restaurant critic. Asked to write honest, amusing reviews, I soon clashed with colleagues who were wary of publishing anything that might be confused with opinion. The experience was bizarre, immensely disconcerting. Rattled, I left the paper, fled to Morocco, and then to the west of Ireland. There I began to consider the function of critics, and the fate of Kola Boof, over spicy chicken wings in a barbecue sauce.

This wandering account is an attempt to put some sense on the following summer, which ended with a month in the wilderness. Perhaps I should have stayed there. This is a declaration of ignorance, and, eventually, of intent. Most of the action occurs in my mind, but it helps, I suppose, to recall what was, or was not, happening in the real world.

With its opening dream sequence, *Fahrenheit 9/11* captured the mood of the moment. Millions marveled at Michael Moore's rant, and the critics said his new documentary was more mature than *Bowling for Columbine,* which I could not understand. It was like saying that Frosties are more intelligent than Rice Krispies.

George W. Bush was running for reelection. The White House upped the panic levels to orange: the second-highest state of national alert. John Kerry promised to do something about it, and no one was quite sure what he meant. In the absence of reliable information, conspiracy theories gained new credibility. At a dinner party, a middle-aged woman told me that the Pakistani army had captured Osama bin Laden. "He will be unveiled just before the election," she predicted. "Bush will win, of course. Six months later, Pakistan's trade deficit will mysteriously shrink."

It is often said that Christmas starts earlier each year. Have you noticed that the silly season gets longer? A few days after I returned from Roundstone, a friend who works in a national newspaper rang up to ask if I had any news. "I'll take anything," he said. "We're just desperate for something that readers might take seriously." Then he started boasting about the special edition of the paper that he had helped to prepare for the death of the pope.

"But the pope is still alive."

"Yes, I know," he said, agitated. "But when he pops . . ."

Then something happened. It was not what you might call important in the autumn, but in the torpor of July it constituted news. Shocked by the childhood obesity epidemic, a slim and youthful Ronald McDonald announced that he was going to make some fitness videos. A spokesman for Ronald revealed that the "high-energy entertainment series" (*Buns of Steel?*) would feature "original songs and fun adventures that will get kids on their feet, actively participating."

Here was a man with a long history of improbable victory. First, he convinced a large multinational corporation to hire a clown as its public face. Then he squeezed kitsch into kitchen. In time, he would crash thousands of kids' birthday parties without receiving a single threat of incarceration. And now he was going to teach tubby tots *how to clap their hands.*

Ronald's new mission — an act, I assumed, of monumental cynicism — got me thinking. If McDonald's is so concerned about the effect that fast food has on children, why doesn't it produce food that improves their health? We know that excessive amounts of salt, sugar, and fat are not part of the life well lived. Why don't the good guys at McDonald's do something meaningful about the tragedy-in-waiting that is the health of their youngest customers? Why make *a fitness video?*

A few days later, in one of those apparent coincidences that later comes to define an era in one's mind, I was invited to a preview screening of *Super Size Me,* a documentary about food in the tradition of Michael Moore. I had read about *Super Size Me,* had heard about it from friends in New York, and could hardly decline an invitation. At the time, I thought this book was ready to be published.

The premise of the film is straightforward: in a bid to chart the effects of fast food on the human body, Morgan Spurlock eats nothing but McDonald's food for a month — breakfast, lunch, and dinner. He becomes quite fat. ("No shit, Spurlock," quipped one critic. "Also, dude, the sky is blue.") Hypertension, high cholesterol, and a lard-ass are all recycled as selling points for art. Watching the film, I had the impression that its star would eat *anything* for a headline.

Morgan Spurlock touches on some interesting subjects: corporate responsibility versus personal responsibility; marketing and its power; obesity; the ubiquity of the golden arches. Then he embarks on a mad crusade to expand his girth, proving nothing but the fact that there really is one born every minute. When Spurlock puts on weight, the audience is supposed to sit back and gasp in disgust. Not me. I simply marveled at the man's ambition. How could anyone be that desperate to get on television?

McDonald's never suggested that anyone should eat its products morning, noon, and night. To absolve itself of precisely the charge that Spurlock levels, it stresses that a Big Mac, say, can be enjoyed *as part of* a healthy diet. Call it verbal sleight of hand: instead of encouraging us to see the bigger picture about what we consume — far too much saturated fat, sugar, and salt — everything is billed as a one-off incident. No food is bad per se. (Don't worry about the hydrogenated fats in that bar of chocolate either: no one died after eating one Mars bar.) This semantic device is often used to get fast-food companies off the hook, but on this occasion it's well founded. *Super Size Me* is predicated on the risible view that some people, somewhere, must eat at McDonald's all the time.

Super Size Me was irritating, but it was also embarrassing. Watching it, I reflected on the message at the heart of this book: a food critic doesn't need to cook, so ignorance is somehow acceptable; anyone can review restaurants. And never mind the danger of consuming or promoting a lot of unhealthy food; dining out rocks.

I blushed. A lot.

The following day, I left the office for lunch at ten to one. But I didn't come back. I went away. To Connemara, once again. I have always liked that part of the country. Remote enough to deter the stag parties that descend on Dublin, it is also wild enough — truly wild, that is — to encourage contemplation. I wanted to finish this book, but I didn't. I read and I cooked. At home, I seldom get a chance to do either. (Epicures may sigh at that disclosure. Anyone who has struggled to get a business off the ground will not.) It was the first time in two or three years that I had chopped an onion. It was the first time since devouring *Fast Food Nation* that I had sat down to read books about food. They weren't cookbooks; they were manifestos, by the sort of people who would hate my own for being so pleased with its ignorance, and for those two fingers jauntily raised to chefs. *All* chefs.

My head was full of orange alerts and Morgan Spurlock and Michael Moore and the power of polemic, but also its failure to reflect truth, which is often complex, inconvenient. I was thinking about style and substance. I was thinking, too, about food as a thing in itself, possibly rare and usually processed, with a past and a method of production, not as something that might be good this month, though it may fall out of fashion soon. When you eat in restaurants a lot, you lose a sense of the journey from field to plate. You think of sauces that may not work, or of presentation. Price is an issue. I like to eat in comfort. Service, too, becomes a concern. How depressing it is that I should be more concerned about the way that food is offered to me than the manner in which it is grown or raised or culled or killed. How pathetic it is that I have become the sort of person who is more interested in style than substance.

I read with a vague intention to reacquaint myself with issues raised, and then ignored, in Spurlock's film: overdone tracts on diet, a brilliant polemic about the supermarket industry (*Shopped,* by Joanna Blythman), best-selling tomes on the effect of everyday food, sensationalist rubbish, grimacing takes on Atkins woe. All quite interesting, often well intentioned.

After two weeks in the wilderness, I could not dispute Dr. Johnson's right to fault a wonky table. "You can scold a carpenter who has made you a bad table," he said, "though you cannot make a table. It is not your trade to make tables." Perhaps it was the combined effect of all those terror alerts, my sautéed skate, and the absence of anything one might call news. No sign of bin Laden, and nothing ever happens in the west of Ireland. Connemara is slightly unreal. Stranger still, this book made sense. It is true that everyone is entitled to criticize a meal in public, and anyone who insists that such a job should be left to experts is but a snob.

It could have ended there. I could have allowed myself to finish the trip with a smug repetition of first principles. But I knew, too, that I had to take responsibility for my own opinions, examine the implications. I also had to assess the role of restaurants in a wider context: as an arm of the food business. I wrote a survey of the way we eat today — noted the contradictions, expressed alarm, yet failed to consider my complicity. I avoided doing this, and it does not serve my case, or the case of this book, to do so any longer. I must explore. Otherwise I'm no different to Morgan Spurlock, the man who complained that McDonald's would have answered his questions if only he'd been Michael Moore. I do not want to be described as a poor man's poor man's Michael Moore.

*　　*　　*

Food has never been less expensive or more convenient. Twenty-five years ago, Britons spent, on average, an hour in the kitchen preparing each main meal. Today it takes twenty minutes to do the same job. In 1934, 23 percent of the disposable income of the average American was spent on food at home. Today that figure is 7 percent. Unfortunately, those statistics take no account of quality: children consume more than their body weight in French fries every nine months, and the British now eat more ready meals than the rest of Europe put together. How did we get to this point? And who is to blame?

Malnutrition is the great disgrace of the age, and in its shadow all discussion about the difference between good food and bad food seems almost tasteless. I want to know if it is possible to justify the consumption of expensive food at a time when humans continue to starve to death. First, however, I want to look at the manner in which the rich world eats, for we are also witnessing an increase in diseases of overnutrition, or a new kind of malnutrition based on diets that are high in calories but relatively low in nutrients: stroke, high blood pressure, diabetes, and heart disease. I suspect the food industry knows that it is "habituating" children to a profoundly unhealthy diet. Is that true? And, if so, am I right to be disturbed?

Or is everything under control?

At the time of the Renaissance, most Europeans consumed about one teaspoon of sugar a year. There are seven teaspoons of sugar in a can of Coca-Cola. Salt? Many of the most popular processed foods, like bread, baked beans, and pizza, are full of the stuff. Then there is saturated fat. We can't get enough meat and dairy products. Why? Will we never learn?

We are certainly blind to the fate of animals, and that includes ourselves. Eating fish that is farmed, dyed, and de-sexed is a typical symptom of modern myopia. I prefer the sight of antlers on a wall — less critical of the age than of human nature. We admire the wilderness, but also regard it as a dangerous place to be colonized. This pose has sustained the species since the dawn of civilization. It may now be enough to kill us all. "We don't see animals raised," writes the journalist Adam Nicolson. "We don't see the connection between the meat and the animal of which it formed a part. We don't know the people who are selling the food to us, nor they us, except insofar as their marketing survey might identify us as a member of one consumer group or another. Individuality of relations has been burnt away. We are vacuum-packed."

In an assignment for the *New Yorker,* Bill Buford once spent seventy-two hours watching the Food Network. At the end of it, he wrote, "I couldn't recall very many potatoes with dirt on them, or beets with ragged greens, or carrots with soil in their creases, or pieces of meat remotely reminiscent of the animals they were butchered from — hardly anything, it seemed, from planet Earth."

Perhaps there is no reason to regard such information with disdain. In Connemara, I read an essay by Michael Lind, a senior fellow at the New America Foundation. Lind talks about our moral imperative to ensure that "all people on Earth enjoy the nutritional benefits of the meat-rich Paleolithic diet of the upper classes." He rubbishes the idea that affluent countries should revert to "the unhealthy peasant diet" and predicts a future in which new strains of crops will be more resistant to pests and will require few or no fertilizers. People who object to "Frankenfoods" can relax, says Lind, there are technical fixes for all our problems. Smart breeding — a kind of traditional breeding aided by computer analysis — "can accomplish many of the same results of more direct genetic engineering," allowing large tracts of land to be returned to nature.

Science is not necessarily the enemy. The potential benefits of genetically modified crops in the poor world are huge, which is part of the reason why even the Vatican is undecided about their use. At the moment, however, many experts suspect that they ask more questions than they answer, and when Lind goes on to advocate tissue-cloning techniques for growing portions of meat by themselves, one imagines that he may have a good sense of humor. The "food snobs" who want free-range chicken are, says Lind, "enemies of the biosphere." The way forward is not to return to traditional methods of farming, but to embrace science. "As the owner of a small ranch in Texas," he argues, "I can attest that a pasture and a cow is an extremely inefficient way to convert soil, water, and sunlight into a steak. I would rather eat a nutritious pork chop from a clean laboratory test tube than from a pig which had spent its life drugged in a tiny cage caked with its own waste."

In excluding the middle, by suggesting that there are only two choices in the matter, Michael Lind does his own argument a disservice. This is the logic of the schoolyard bully. "It makes no sense," he writes, "to counsel individuals and nations to adopt austerity in cases in which there are technological solutions to problems created by technology." Lind uses the word *austerity* in the same way that George W. Bush uses the word *liberal*. It is not a mark of respect. But there is nothing wrong with exercising responsibility in our governance of the planet. We have already done quite a lot of plundering. All that happy talk of "growing" chicken breasts? Forget it. There are too many reasons to be skeptical about the food we eat already, and free-range chicken is not one of them.

Look at the achievements of Lind's friends, who have synthesized thousands of new chemicals. These are things which never existed before, of which all living organisms — including, of course, humans — have no evolutionary experience. They are sold as herbicides, pesticides, and fungicides to food producers, precisely because they kill weeds, insects, and fungi. We are assured by the vacuous blondes who front food companies that the residues are perfectly safe. Unconvinced. The testing of chemicals is expensive; you cannot find what you don't look for; you can't carry out experiments on humans in the way that is done with lab animals; and, above all, the tests don't last very long. We know nothing about the long-term effects of most dietary changes. I want my body to last for eighty years. It would be convenient if the environment also survived.

Alarmed by what I had read, I phoned an expert in food policy. Rosalind Sharpe told me about the omnivore's paradox: the ability of humans to adapt our diet to anything available has helped us to survive — unlike, say, pandas, which die out as their sole source of food, the bamboo forests, disappear. Unfortunately, this versatility has also left us with no in-built aversion to foods that may harm us. Now I was scared.

Food Fascism: Facts and Fiction

Who are the real "food fascists"? The murky figures behind that term may be a more insidious threat to democracy than anyone who cares about food. Posing as friends of freedom, AstroTurf (faux grass-roots) advocacy groups attack anyone who dares to question the right to peddle junk food. As Michael Pollan, author of *The Omnivore's Dilemma*, wrote recently, "Many of the same groups that Big Tobacco launched to attack its critics have seamlessly moved into attacking the critics of Big Food. This is hardly a coincidence: large segments of the food industry share corporate parents with Big Tobacco."

Such advocacy groups deny "that food, like tobacco, is a public-health issue that demands public education and action." And they make no apology for ad hominem attacks on the "Food Police," for the intention has always been to shoot the messenger. Meanwhile, the media — headline-friendly, or keen to placate advertisers — has blithely co-opted the term, thus endorsing the myth that critics of agribusiness are mere busybodies, interfering with our right to consume its junk.

Big Food promotes itself as a defender of basic freedoms, unlike its "harsh" and "repressive" critics. So the billions of dollars that fast-food companies spend on marketing represent not control but freedom. Yet, as Pollan observes: "This marketing involves the routine manipulation of children — bribing them with toys, enticing them to eat more with cleverly designed packaging and portion sizes, and deploying the arts of food science to exploit their inborn cravings for fat, salt, and sugar. So who exactly is the more 'controlling' party here?"

The companies that decry litigation against the food industry thought nothing of suing Oprah Winfrey for suggesting that there might be mad cow disease in the U.S. beef supply, or of lobbying Congress to grant the industry immunity from obesity lawsuits. In their cynical attempts to stymie debate, it is not a love of freedom that one detects, but something darker and less democratic. One begins to imagine that the real "food fascists" are the people who coined that term.

★   ★   ★

The incidence of obesity has quadrupled in Britain in the last twenty-five years. In America, it will soon overtake smoking as the main preventable cause of death. After a long conversation about the role of big business in all this, Rosalind Sharpe offered to send me some information about processed foods. Full of the stuff *we're supposed to avoid* — fat, sugar, salt — they already comprise nearly four-fifths of our diet. That proportion is likely to increase, explained Sharpe, "pulled by consumers' demand for convenience and value and pushed by producers' desire to add value to raw materials — in other words, to sell crisps [potato chips] rather than raw potatoes, thus earning a much higher return per kilo of raw material."

Ronald McDonald and the vacuous blonde are figureheads. Listening to them, one has no sense of the size, power, and ambition of the firms for which they daily spin. Processed food includes everything from canned pasta to those lucrative ready meals that you see in every supermarket. Most of the ingredients are the sort of thing that you would never expect to find in a domestic kitchen. "Put crudely," explained Sharpe, "quite a lot of it involves making different combinations of generic ingredients like fat, protein, sweetness, or starch, from interchangeable sources, with palatability, flavor, appearance, texture, and preservability designed in by food scientists."

Quality is sacrificed to cost in many industries, but the notion that the flavor and texture of dinner is "designed in by food scientists" makes me nauseous. The food industry claims that it is driven by demand and produces things because we want them. But no one asked for sticks of processed orange cheese (Cheese Strings). So manufacturers are creating demand, as well as simply responding to it. We can't really ask them to stop. Or can we?

If humans are serious about tackling the damage that unhealthy food does to us, some commentators argue that we should simply be fussier about what we eat — exercise personal responsibility. Speaking to the *Observer Food Monthly* in 2005, Henrietta Green, the original champion of farmers' markets, issued a plea to consumers: "If you're terrified of Tesco and the way it is eroding our core values, then don't bloody shop there." At the end of *Fast Food Nation,* Eric Schlosser's exposé of the junk-food business, the author issues a similar appeal:

> Nobody in the United States is forced to buy fast food. The first step toward meaningful change is by far the easiest: stop buying it. The executives who run the fast-food industry are not bad men. They are businessmen. They will sell free-range, organic, grass-fed hamburgers if you demand it. They will sell whatever sells at a profit. The usefulness of the market, its effectiveness as a tool, cuts both ways. The real power of the American consumer has not yet been unleashed. The heads of Burger King, KFC, and McDonald's should feel daunted: they're outnumbered. There are three of them and almost three hundred million of you. A good boycott, a refusal to buy, can speak much louder than words. Sometimes the most irresistible force is the most mundane.

If, like me, you read *Fast Food Nation* with a mounting sense of rage, you probably relished those lines. However, Schlosser's noble sentiment is undermined by a fact that few seem prepared to accept: in the West, people are gluttonous. That observation is born of experience (my stomach on the march) and supported by research. Loyd Grossman★ and Paul Newman have convinced the public to buy in their likenesses, but no government has yet convinced us to eat sensibly. It seems that indulgence is hardwired into our genes. Conversely, when we deign to buy unprocessed foods, we vote with our eyes — "normal"-shaped spuds, fruit that sparkles — but not with our taste buds. This encourages food producers to use coloring and additives.

At a recent round-table discussion organized by the *New Statesman,* the U.K. minister for public health, Caroline Flint, claimed that

---

★I interviewed Loyd Grossman for this book. "What about the role of big food in this," I asked him, "namely, those companies that supply us with foods high in salt, sugar, and saturated fats? How can we persuade such companies to stop flogging foods that are obviously bad for our health?" Grossman's response: "Well, that sort of thing has nothing to do with restaurants. Therefore, I wouldn't have a view on that when talking in the context of restaurants."

72 percent of eleven- to sixteen-year-olds understand the importance of a healthy diet. During the same discussion, Paul Lincoln, the chief executive of the British National Heart Forum, predicted that 50 percent of British children will be obese by 2020. In reply, Melanie Leech of the Food and Drink Federation trotted out the industry shtick — "[We] respond to consumer demand" — before claiming that she, like everyone else, would love to see children eating a balanced diet. There was, however, a caveat: ". . . That starts by equipping children to make those healthy choices. If you focus on individual foods and individual choices, you run the risk of creating a situation in which people become deficient in essential nutrients."

There is something almost farcical about a representative of the food industry claiming that attempts to improve the quality of the nation's diet may deprive us of essential nutrients. But Big Food has no monopoly on myopia. Let us admit what Melanie Leech, R. J. Nabisco, Philip Morris, Morgan Spurlock, and even Eric Schlosser cannot get their heads around. Personal responsibility won't cut it, and even when manufacturers tell people what they're really eating — this has started to happen in certain states — it does not make sufficient difference. Some of us are just too busy or indulgent, or busy *and* indulgent, to take much notice. The rest of us are motivated by price alone.

So what can we do?

To allay the damage that dinner now poses, we could lobby the food industry to remove some of the salt, fat, and sugar in popular products. Problem: what company would voluntarily do anything that puts its profits at risk? As a society, we could equip ourselves to make more informed choices about the food we consume. (Anyone who writes about food, even if it is just restaurant food, has an opportunity to contribute to that discussion.) We could lobby the government to take a far more active role in determining what sort of messages we receive about food. And finally, if that doesn't work, we could ask the government to punish those companies that seem so keen to make us fat and sick.

★   ★   ★

Maybe you think all this too sanguine, or just naive. Some of the proposals would be difficult, if not impossible, to implement (some are on the way). A many-headed monster with a massive advertising budget, the food industry has a powerful hold on mass media, and it has weapons that are the match of even the most sincere politician. One of those weapons is disinformation. Many public-health experts now believe that the food industry is deliberately keeping us in a state of confusion about what food is good and bad for us. They want us to think that nothing we do makes any difference and thus abandon any efforts to change the way we eat.

Ten Ways to Tackle Mad-Chow Disease

1. **Convince supermarkets to give consumers loyalty points for healthy foods.** Consumers would have more money to spend on food as a result of purchasing healthier items.

2. **Teach food and cooking in a hands-on way.** So children are encouraged to consider the provenance of ingredients and start to enjoy cooking at a young age.

3. **Ban advertising for unhealthy food.** In 2004, $260 million was spent on advertising by Britain's top-ten food and drink companies. The government spent $2 million promoting healthy eating. The message is not making any impact.

4. **Ban food advertisements from children's television.**

5. **Remove vending machines from schools.** Soft-drink and confectionery companies pay schools to farm for new customers — far less than the government will spend in treating the consequences of obesity in the future.

6. **Advertise more.** To counter the influence of junk-food advertising, use the same techniques to promote healthy options. In some U.S. states, tobacco firms must pay for anti-smoking ads.

(continued)

Ten Ways to Tackle Mad-Chow Disease *(cont.)*

7. **Subsidize corner shops to sell more fresh produce.** Or subsidize independent butchers. We already subsidize farmers who want to grow — or not grow — certain crops.

8. **Introduce a nutrient tax.** Apply it to saturated fat and sugar. Or put VAT on milk. A 2004 report in the British Medical Journal argued that if VAT was extended to whole milk, butter, and cheese — the main sources of saturated fat — nearly 1,000 deaths could be prevented each year.

9. **Rewrite the Common Agricultural Policy.** Livestock farming receives the bulk of support. Imagine if public health was the priority, rather than the interests of the meat industry.

10. **Oblige food manufacturers to lower levels of salt, fat, and sugar, and/or add vitamins.**

Advertising and public relations are also employed as weapons — to promote lavish claims and to silence dissent. In their book, *Toxic Sludge Is Good for You,* John Stauber and Sheldon Rampton chart the ways that large food companies undermine critics. The PR firm Ketchum, for instance, launched an anti-publicity campaign against David Steinman's *Diet for a Poisoned Planet* in order to ensure that the general public wouldn't learn about the contaminants in California Dancing Raisins, while the author of *Beyond Beef,* Jeremy Rifkin, was the victim of a burglar who broke into his home and stole the schedule for his book tour. A few days later, a woman, posing as the book's publicist, started to cancel his television and radio appearances.

Such events encourage paranoia. However, on the day I left the west of Ireland, I felt almost optimistic. I had just finished reading a book by Colin Tudge, who spent thirty years writing on agriculture, conservation, genetics, and evolution before bringing it all together in a work that is popular science, social history, and foodie manifesto. In *So Shall We Reap,* Tudge documents how the relentless drive for maximum food production at rock-bottom cost has put an end to traditional farming. He reveals the astonishing greed of large corporations, the power of the meat industry, its contempt for animal life, and the bad husbandry that leads to diseases like BSE. He also explores the ways in which our demand for foods rich in sugar, fat, and salt has been manipulated by unscrupulous manufacturers. Reading the book, one is left with the impression that its author would be a terrible dinner-party guest, and that is what I love about his writing. Consider, for instance, Bush's position on climate change: the U.S. president is reluctant to do anything that might upset his patrons or inhibit the domestic economy. Another writer might express frustration. For Colin Tudge, "this is anarchy on a global scale, far more frightening than the terrorism that has launched a thousand warplanes."

The man is obviously a doom-monger. So where is the good news? Well, after exposing the avarice of Big Food, Tudge recommends that you and I should probably go out to dinner. Seriously.

> Good farming provides the kinds of food that are nutritionally perfect, and which also support the world's greatest cuisines. In short, if the world took its lead from good farmers and good cooks, and if science was content to serve those traditional crafts, humanity would have nothing at all to worry about. It's only the economists and politicians who are screwing things up — they and the scientists who have so complaisantly flocked to their cause.
>
> All we really need to do to put world farming back on course, cure and prevent the nutritional disasters of modern humanity, ensure that our descendants are well fed forever, and eat like gourmets, is to take food and cooking seriously.

I interview chefs all the time. They invariably boast about how traditional, organic, or honest their cooking is, how they only use locally sourced, top-notch produce. For a long time, I was skeptical about those claims. However, if even a few chefs are sincerely committed to local ingredients and regional cooking, which is what they all say, then restaurants may be a vital front in the food wars.

Great restaurants are wasteful places, where good food becomes slop and dishes fetch multiples of their true value. Some of us use dining rooms in the way that a certain sort of woman uses department stores: to run away from our own problems — which is fine. Good hospitality can bolster a myth that life is much as it should be. My brief, unwieldy introduction to the politics of food production left me convinced that we could do better. A lot better. If we continue to assault the planet, the biodiversity that makes eating such a pleasure will become a source of mere nostalgia. In taking gastronomy seriously, preserving culinary traditions, and promoting sound farming practices, good chefs are a boon to the species — one reason why expensive restaurants may be more *moral* than is commonly assumed.★

That observation does not make it easy to reconcile famine and fancy food, but it does suggest that it is possible.

What about Ronald McDonald? Isn't he doing the world some service? Those exercise videos must have cost a fortune. In America, where 90 percent of kids eat at McDonald's every month, more playgrounds are operated by the company than by any other private entity. In Australia, a survey revealed that half of nine- and ten-year-olds think Ronald "knows what kids should eat." What does that tell us about this lovable clown?

It tells us that Ronald is one zealous motherfucker.

Societal norms change as experience and statistics conspire to rob us of ignorance. Until recently, it was neither illegal nor socially unacceptable to leave a party and drive home tipsy without wearing a seat belt. A year ago, the Irish dining room was enveloped in a fog of cigarette smoke. (There were smoking sections in some restaurants, just as there are in America, but they were largely ignored or ineffective.) Even smokers admit that the experience of dining out has become

---

★There are other reasons. For instance, spending large amounts of money on food is a relatively sustainable way to exhaust one's income: more sustainable, for instance, than flying to Prague for the weekend or buying an SUV. It is arguable that the more money you spend on food, the more sustainable you become, because the food is then likely to be sourced locally and produced organically.

more pleasant since the introduction of the smoking ban. Problems can only be ignored for so long before governments are obliged to intervene on our behalf. Today, there is a tension between the advice of dietary experts (broadly speaking: eat less) and the constant exhortations of the food business (eat more now, tonight, always). Something has to give.

The founder of the Slow Food movement, Carlo Petrini, once wrote, "A firm defense of quiet material pleasure is the only way to oppose the universal folly of fast life . . . Our defense should begin at the table." City Boy had to go to the country to discover the meaning of Slow Food. Perhaps it is time for Petrini's manifesto, with its calm insistence on local, seasonal produce, to become a best-seller, just as Michelin-starred chefs, those winged Olympians, start to question the system that has made them well-fed slaves and the French admit that food in a restaurant is very important, but rarely as memorable as the sleepy smile of a waitress who wants to follow you home.

Now leaving the wilderness, I am conscious that a bad cook can judge a meal. Greenhorns serve a purpose; expert views are often expressed in opaque language, and intuitive calls are sometimes the most accurate, as the *New Yorker* journalist Malcolm Gladwell revealed in *Blink,* a book-length homage to snap judgments. However, that argument demands appendage. A critic must have concern about, and passion for, the thing he judges; consideration seems hollow in the absence of love. Is it necessary to know *everything* about food? No. Should one obsess about the provenance of each ingredient? No. Should all risk be removed from eating? No. But restaurant critics can ill afford to ignore what's on the plate, or wear ignorance as a badge of honor.

It used to be said that retailers are the gatekeepers of the stomach. As more of us choose to eat in public, consuming more food made by strangers, prepared in conditions that are often questionable, restaurants demand closer inspection. Journalists have a common enemy — people who produce and sell bad food — and a responsibility to expose their shameful antics. In championing my right to slate a meal in a way that was lazy and careless, I have neglected that responsibility.

There are food writers who are conscious of a battle looming. "The food industry has sold us a couple of very dangerous ideas," said Joanna Blythman recently. "The first is that we don't have time to cook, so we should buy processed, pre-prepared foods. The second is that if you do have time to cook, then you must be stuck away in the backwaters of modern life. It's a status symbol not to cook." That comment is a damning critique of the Oliver Twist — eat more, cook less — the paradox that I announced with a chuckle. But Blythman's focus is rare.

What have I done? Where was my focus? The self-deception implicit in the casting of Jamie Oliver as culinary savior, which I revealed in chapter 2, is followed in that same chapter by a PR campaign for the dogs of dinner. More entertaining than erudite, loud without being important, they give much publicity to an industry that cannot bring itself to acknowledge their value. But most have no time for the politics of food production. With lunch as the pretext for a new blood sport, the subject is either overlooked or belittled. That self-deception extends to the coalition of vested interests behind the grandiose claim that London is the restaurant capital of the world. As Blythman observes in *Bad Food Britain,* "People attempting to mount a convincing case for Britain's supposedly rehabilitated food culture have become adept at drawing a veil over the cooking (or lack of it) that goes on in the domestic sphere. They prefer not to focus on the nation's growing daily dependence on push-button industrial food."

It is not always easy or desirable to address some of the wider issues in the context of a restaurant review. Accepted. However, many critics have become part of the story, instead of observing and reporting the bigger story, while figures like Tudge and Blythman are dismissed as eccentrics or caricatured in glib references to the nanny state and food fascism. (It is easy to drive home drunk.)

I finally understand what Craig Claiborne of the *New York Times* meant when he said that the news element is vital in any story about food. Without it, he warned, one is left with "the God-awful pretension and solipsism that trivializes the entire subject and can only, in the end, compromise the reporter." Claiborne said that over thirty years ago, but he could have been referring to the media today.

Most food critics do not just ignore the need to regard all restaurants as an arm of the food business, with the obligations implied by that conclusion. They actively discourage it. At a seminar on the politics of food production a few days before the British edition of this book was launched, Colman Andrews, then editor of *Saveur,* lambasted my suggestion that food critics should pay McDonald's as much attention as Michelin. Foodies are an intemperate bunch — old news — so the attack itself was not, perhaps, surprising. But the rationale? Shocking.

Even the *New York Times* (front-page headline, October 2006: "Entrees Break the $40 Barrier!") has encouraged a glib acceptance that restaurants are in some way unrelated to the food industry. They belong, rather, in the realm of entertainment, and attempts to square the moral and political dimensions of dining out are sometimes unsuccessful, as we shall see in the next chapter.

I returned to Dublin at the beginning of September. The pope was still alive, the newspapers were still full of inane prattle, Osama bin Laden was still at large, America was still on orange alert, and George W. Bush was still on course for reelection. *Super Size Me* was on general release. Vast pictures of its star, his mouth full of chips, were plastered on billboards all over the city. I couldn't get away from Morgan Spurlock. He followed me around for weeks. It felt like a punishment for everything I'd failed to say and do. In a way, I suppose, it was.

At the end of September, I woke up one morning with a phrase fully formed on my lips. "It wasn't a coincidence." I'd been dreaming about Morgan Spurlock, about all those posters, and about the timing of the announcement that McDonald's was going to make some fitness videos, so that kids might learn to clap their hands. Suddenly I realized that, for all my quibbles, Morgan Spurlock is part of the solution.

"*I love the way you make those yams. You'll have to give me the recipe before your culture is obliterated from the face of the earth.*"

13

In Defense of
Expensive Restaurants

The Author Puts On Weight

We must learn to be guests of each other.

— George Steiner

WHEN FINANCIAL WIZARDS GO OFF TO CELEBRATE SOME NEW shafting, they typically demand "the finest wines known to humanity." That means grandstand marques like Lafite and Margaux. New money and old wine go together like cafés and dirty toilets. Young men who don't know anything about claret demand magnums of the stuff that oenophiles describe as precious nectar.

When journalists write about these sixty-grand lunches, a question is implied, if rarely put in such elitist terms: How dare the philistines spend so much money *on something they clearly don't get*? Wine lovers nod in bitter agreement, while readers who regard themselves as prudent resent such extravagance on the basis that others have so little. In the case of the wine lover, the hack, and the puritan, there is a certain amount of jealousy at play, and often a little hypocrisy.

When the Vatican intervenes, as it once did, to describe a $4,000 meal as "scandalous," one cannot resist a titter.

Bad food is bad value, no matter what it costs. Besides, there is nothing more natural than going out to dinner for a slap-up meal. "Scandalous" is a good word to describe the fact that lots of fat, rich people think that the problems of a great many poor, hungry people have nothing to do with them. Confused? But of course. You live in a world in which (a) humans suffer malnutrition on an epic scale, and (b) it is possible to spend over $800 for one dinner in one New York restaurant. As a reader of the *Sunday Times* once put it in a letter to Michael Winner, "In the midst of genocide, famine, earthquake and war, I can always be assured of your vacuous discussion of an unknown restaurant, a description of some bizarre potato dish and a picture of you, scarlet face, apparently intoxicated and surrounded by bemused staff."

Confusion is quite different from falling victim to the shibboleth that we are powerless. Some people — like journalists, politicians, and, for some reason, pop stars — exert a disproportionate influence on world affairs, but if recent events have taught us anything it is that remote, unaccountable powers are not invulnerable to public opinion. In chapter 13, I noted that people in the rich world are unlikely to act in unison to improve the quality of the food we eat. We can, ironically, come together to improve the conditions in which other humans live. This chapter is supposed to illustrate that point, and, by the way, to argue that eating in expensive restaurants is not as contemptible as prigs suggest.

To prove all this, we need to find someone who straddles the worlds of high living, fine dining, and famine. We need to find someone who might wish to drink too much tonight and feed the world tomorrow. I propose Bono. No better man for a liberal whinge, the U2 singer owns the Clarence, a boutique hotel that boasts one of Dublin's best restaurants. There, diners can buy a bottle of 1999 Screaming Eagle for $4,000. Twelve years ago, the showbiz activist spent a month working in an Ethiopian orphanage.

As a child, I was forced to endure the opinions of Bono, and like everyone in Ireland, I felt aggrieved when someone else was asked to write his biography. There were things, however, that remained unsaid about the most public man in the country. I did not hear about his aid work in Ethiopia until recently. When Bono returned to the country in 2001 with American treasury secretary Paul O'Neill, they were accompanied by several television crews. This part-time activist has always been complex. Perhaps I mean confusing. It is hard to keep up with his radical views on saving the world, singing the blues, and hydroelectric dams. But Bono is certainly astute. "If there's one thing worse than a rock star," he says, "it's a rock star with a conscience."★

Bono thinks the duty of civilized human beings is to tackle the greatest injustice of the day, be it apartheid, slavery or, in our case, the plight of people who are either exploited or neglected by the rich world. "Betray your age," says the man who defines his own.

And such an age. Nearly two-thirds of all British adults are overweight or obese. Eight hundred and forty million humans are officially classified as malnourished because they lack the money to buy food, *despite a global surplus.* Hard to justify but easy to explain, these are surely the facts of an immature species, lacking perspective and unprepared for the subtle challenge of sustainability.

Hardly anyone likes to discuss this subject in public, which is not to suggest that everyone debates it in private. I have read just one defense of the good life by a prominent critic. In a short, jaunty essay, William Grimes of the *New York Times* dares to answer a question that could be asked more often: In a world where millions starve today, how can one justify spending hundreds on dinner tonight?

Arguments against fine dining rest on one of two propositions. The first is utilitarian. In the Malthusian view, the food that we all eat comes out of some big pie, so it is unfair for one of us to eat too

---

★Actors are even worse. On the eve of elections in 2005, Palestinians were subjected to a political broadcast by the star of *Pretty Woman.* "Hi, I'm Richard Gere," he began, "and I'm speaking for the entire world . . "

much. Dismissing this logic, Grimes writes: "No one, rationally, believes in the pie-chart model. Food surpluses pose as much of a problem as food shortages, and famines, it turns out, usually have political causes that require political solutions."

Grimes is right to question utilitarianism. However, the conflation of food shortages with famine is unfortunate, it is debatable whether food surpluses are as damaging as food shortages, and his dismissal of widespread hunger as something with "political" causes and "political" solutions is somewhat chilling. The implication is that you and I have no cause to intervene.

"There is food available," continues Grimes, "but the wrong people, like warlords or autocrats, have wrested control of it." So the baddies have pinched all the food. And there is no connection between big food and the political establishment. A third of all the food produced by the heavily subsidized food industry goes to waste; 86 percent of the Earth's resources are consumed by one-fifth of the world's population: according to William Grimes, these are things that you and I shouldn't bother our little heads about.

This is how Grimes summarizes the second objection to eating in expensive restaurants:

> It is all right to enjoy food, but not too much. It is all right to eat out, but not to spend too much money doing it. There are two moral impulses intertwined here: the ancient prohibition against gluttony and the more puritan objection to indulging pleasure for its own sake.

Noting that this sort of objection is weirdly confined to food — no one grumbles about other people paying hundreds of dollars on tickets for a football match — Grimes says that, for most diners, expensive restaurant meals are a luxury. It is not every day that we spend vast sums on fancy food. Besides, it is probably quite healthy to break a routine. If humans were utterly rational beings, we would eat only what is necessary to sustain ourselves while doing unpleasant, dutiful things like putting out the garbage or taking our in-laws seriously. But we're not just rational beings, which is why we demand cakes and ale. Given a choice, says Grimes, we'll "opt for a cherry on the top of the cake too."

Here he is on much safer ground. It is foolish to argue against indulgence. Look at Bono. It may seem grotesque that a liberal advocate of global justice would sell, or consume, a bottle of wildly expensive grape juice. And you may think it rich of Bono to lecture G8 leaders on their obligations to the poor. ("Rock stars," sighs Homer Simpson. "Is there anything they don't know?") In fact, if he did not live it up a bit, we wouldn't take Bono seriously. Consider for a moment how preposterous the millionaire would appear in sackcloth and ashes. We would not expect him to give away all his worldly possessions before daring to speak of poverty, and we realize at some level that ascetics are not the only people qualified to express concern about the state of the world. What we rarely admit, however, is that to be unyielding in one's application of a principle can actually be a sign of madness.★

Sometimes, I feel obliged to put a lid on my enjoyment because others do not share my good fortune. "The greatest good for the greatest number" is an attractive principle. But among the implications of utilitarianism is the idea that we have an obligation to make other people happy. If you follow this logic to its conclusion, you must

---

★Humans cherish constancy, but we do not think about its consequences with any rigor. In *Zig Zag: The Politics of Culture and Vice Versa,* the German writer Hans Magnus Enzensberger argues that consistency will turn any good cause into a bad one. Do you think that sounds ludicrous? Are you *certain* that it's ludicrous? "Attack the social system you live in by any means at your disposal, and you have terrorism; defend it by any means, and you have a Gestapo running the place. Be a rigorous ecologist and defend nature against man with no holds barred, and you will end up leading a Stone Age existence. Pursue economic growth at any price, and you will destroy the biosphere. Join the arms race, be consistent about it, and you will blow yourself to pieces." Eventually, one concludes, perhaps a little humbly, that consistency is not the only yardstick by which the achievements of a man should be measured. The three most consistent politicians of the twentieth century were Hitler, Stalin, and Pol Pot.

spend all your time, money, and energy in pursuit of that goal. The tale is often told of a wealthy industrialist who became an obsessive act utilitarian. After giving away all his money, he felt morally bound to go even further, so he gave up one of his kidneys to someone he had never met. It is deeply counterintuitive to view such actions as obligations.

Addressing the same issue, Steve Russell, a therapist and journalist who calls himself the Barefoot Doctor, once argued in *The Observer* that the more pleasure you let yourself feel, the more you can share, thus increasing the stock of happiness and goodwill. It seems almost impudent to reflect on the inner monologue of the well-fed diner, and on one level such devotion to pleasure appears similarly deluded. However, the man may have a point:

> When you limit your joy, this only serves to accentuate the subsequent sorrow as joy fades, simply because you didn't get your money's worth and are left deprived and regretful as well. In fact, I'd say it is your existential duty, in honour of the invisible realm whence springs both sorrow and joy, to stretch wide the receptacle and take in as much joy as possible — if only because the more joy you're able to experience, the more joy you're able to share with others, which is ultimately your highest function here on the planet.

It seems that breaking a routine is no bad thing, and extracting pleasure from life is a good way to provoke the same sensation elsewhere. Love begets love. My problem with the essay in the *New York Times* is that the author neglects to make the link between "us" and "them." His world is large enough to accommodate politicians and autocrats, but there is a clear distinction in the article between these grand forces and little old you: "Food is a convenient way for ordinary people to experience extraordinary pleasure, to live it up a bit." That same privilege is not extended to "ordinary people" in much of sub-Saharan Africa, where living it up is rather more difficult.

It is natural to go out to expensive restaurants, not exceptional nor hypocritical nor unreasonable. Attempts to improve our lot are judged according to their efficacy, and my failure to dine at the Clarence tonight will not do the world much good. There are greater gestures, more effective actions. What *is* unreasonable is that we should do nothing all the time. As moral agents, with some intelligence and the power to influence public events, it is incumbent upon us to spend some — but not all — of our time and, yes, our money, in a bid to relieve suffering elsewhere. But to do so all the time — or, indeed, to spend all of our money, like the committed act utilitarian — would not be a sign of compassion, but of madness.

Let us be clear: when we consistently ignore the plight of other humans, we belittle ourselves in the process. Part of the reason why those claret-swilling yuppies invite our scorn is because we know nothing else about them. If it emerged that they holiday in Ethiopia, assisting at an orphanage, or that their time is largely spent lobbying Western leaders to address global injustice, we would regard them in a different light. (Yes, we might also be bloody amazed.) It is not their indulgence that is vulgar. On the contrary, it is their apparent negligence.

We live in a society, not an economy. Its destiny will probably be decided in a row between power and compassion. We need angry heroes to fight our corner, because money talks louder than sense.

It is hard to get it on when you don't know what you're at. Witness the efforts of a major newspaper to justify haute cuisine. Even Bono is accused of getting his priorities wrong, by people who want the same results. After the G8 Summit in 2005, Bianca Jagger said that she felt betrayed by his "moral ambiguity and sound-bite propaganda." By exploiting his own celebrity, Bono exposes himself to the charge of careerism, and yes, there is something laughable about a rock star with a conscience. But harnessing the power of public opinion can make a difference. According to the *Financial Times,* the reason that Japan and Germany supported the historic debt deal in 2005 was not because they wanted to, but because they felt obliged to "bow to the political reality of strong public support for the deal."

That deal was a small victory in a war that is far from over. In the meantime, a great many children will go to bed hungry tonight, *and* you'll need your dinner. Those are difficult things to reconcile. What's more confusing still is that Bono has begun to make sense. It is time, as he says, to betray the age. That means getting involved. There is no better way to plan the next move than over a glass of very good wine.

14

Sex and the Single Waitress

Meeting Mr. Kitchen Confidential

LATE ONE AFTERNOON IN OCTOBER 2004, TOM DOORLEY, THE restaurant critic of the *Irish Times,* rang my office with an invitation.

"I'm round the corner. Fancy dinner on the *Times*?"

A man with some pride might have said, "No, thanks, Tom. There's a two-hour *Simpsons* special on Sky." Ten minutes after the invitation was issued, I met my successor in a hot new *boîte*. The maître d' made no attempt to conceal his shock at seeing us together. I wasn't drinking at the time. A decent skin, Tom kept toasting my sobriety as he regaled me with waspish tales of life as a top-flight restaurant critic. I kept saying, "I know, I know," but Tom was determined to have some fun; I felt asinine for failing to drink my share. Here was a senior colleague — a man who had actually been a teacher in my school — exposing me as a dullard in the middle of the city's most fashionable dining room.

(I cannot remember the food, but the waitress, who was from Irkutsk, said something I shall never forget, in withering response to my invitation to come out for a drink. The sentence did not start with the words, "In Siberia, we do things differently . . . ," but that was the

implication. "It is practical," she announced, "as well as wise, to discover if a woman is sleeping alone, before you apply to share her bed.")

Toward the end of the meal, Tom announced that he was going
to have lunch with Anthony Bourdain.

"Really?" I said, trying to hide my horror.

"Yes, he's here for the day, on a book tour. Tomorrow. Where
should I take him?"

I said the first thing that came into my head and promptly asked,
in the fashion of all hacks on the scrounge (a smile, a whisper, a wink),
to know the name of Bourdain's publisher. My motive was not to lend
this book an imperial ounce of kudos by interviewing the man who
wrote *Kitchen Confidential,* Anthony Bourdain, the hard-living chef
who famously revealed his zany exploits in a New York restaurant
kitchen. And I did not imagine that Tony Bourdain could help me unravel some of the contradictions at the heart of the restaurant racket. I
was jealous.

I did not sense some underlying order in the series of events;
without the *Irish Times,* I wouldn't have written the book this became,
and without this dinner, which the newspaper would pay for, I would
not have met Bourdain. I did not reflect on fate as I cycled at speed to
work the following morning. I thought only of bagging Bourdain. I
too would meet the Lou Reed of Food.

"Too late," said the publicist.

"But I have to meet him. You don't understand . . ."

Much rustling of paper. "I can give you fifteen minutes."

"Excellent. Where?"

"The Clarence. Five fifteen. It's the last interview of the day. And
don't publish anything before next Saturday. I've promised the
Irish Times first dibs."

The Clarence. Bono's hotel. Typical, I thought, smarting, in fact, at that last sentence. I spent the morning reading anything I could find on Bourdain, except, of course, the book of recipes he was here to promote. At lunchtime, I sat at my desk, scouring the Internet and slowly picking at an orange in the manner of that woman who took a pair of scissors to her husband's ties, as she thought of him meeting his lover in some airport hotel.

It was only as I climbed the steps to the hotel, a few minutes after five, that I realized how silly it had been to resent Bourdain and Doorley their meeting. It was all part of some unresolved business. Time to get over it, let go. By coming to this hotel, it was I who was riding on coattails. And it was I who needed the endorsement this meeting might bring.

Good advice to myself in the lobby, the handsome lobby of a beautiful old hotel: "You were lucky to meet Tom last night. Don't be small."

Tony Bourdain is a very cool character. Tall. Handsome. Hip. Funny. As he fluffed another question that it probably wasn't fair to ask, I caught myself admiring him as one might admire a drunken friend impressing some girl on the last bus home with stories that won't lie down. A waitress, probably. I bet he's slept with plenty. Looks like Jeff Goldblum, dresses like Harvey Keitel. You get the impression that he wants to be buried in black leather. Assumes your confidence and speaks as he writes. No great respect for grammar; farrago of clauses, delivered at a pace that implies a tax on time; sounds like he learned to speak English in the kitchen of a very cheap Chinese restaurant in Queens.

Interviewing Tony Bourdain, you sort of want to tell him to slow down, shut up, reconsider, and you admire him all the more for refusing to censor himself. It's the same quality you prize in someone who is prepared to follow the logic of an unpopular political position until it proves itself redundant, or becomes some unvarnished expression of the truth. Rare enough.

There were bags under Bourdain's eyes. Later, I learned that he had arrived from New York at six that morning. This would be his seventh or eighth interview of the day. It was punctuated by two cigarettes in the rain, lasted longer than fifteen minutes, and got off to a clumsy start. I fiddled with the tape recorder, and after some moments of apology, good grace, and further apology, Bourdain signaled to the publicist with a weary sigh that he was just about ready for a pint of Guinness. What about the hack? Care to drink the hotel dry? "Just water," I said, for the second time in two days; a quiet, unplanned act of aggression that was neither wise nor kind. No one likes to drink alone, and I had the impression that the man deserved a pint.

Trevor White (TW): Right, that's it. Sorry. So restaurant criticism is a personal . . .

Anthony Bourdain (AB): I do believe that the star system can be useful, but I would much rather hear about the context. I want to hear what the writer brought to the table, what the experience was like, what the room felt like; that has a lot to do with how the food tastes. I can figure out from that, more often than not, if this is the type of place in which I want to eat.

TW: So the whole idea of impartiality . . . it doesn't exist?

AB: All I look for in a food critic as a chef is that you're not bent, that you're not shaking me down for free food; that you didn't have a bad love affair with my owner, you know, years ago, and you're getting back at her; that you haven't been paid off. If you're not corrupt or evil or ultimately bribed by the competition, then that's really all I can ask.

TW: But don't you think that all bias is a form of corruption? I mean, if I hate the taste of lemon meringue pie, I'm not qualified to . . .

AB: Then *tell me that*. I think if I'm running a restaurant that specializes in lemon meringue pie, or it's my signature dish, then

I think you should refuse yourself for that review. But among many other dishes on the menu, I think you should, perhaps, form a point that you've never liked meringue pie. And I think you should be willing to try it again. I mean, there are some big foods I don't particularly like, some things I don't like at all, but I will try them and I will eat them, again and again.

TW: OK. Do you think the Irish have contributed anything to culinary culture?

AB: Yeah, I think they're contributing a hell of a lot of good seafood and cheese right now.

TW: Seafood and cheese?

AB: Just right off the top of my head. That comes to mind immediately, and I think that will only get better and better. But a lot of damn good cooks use them.

TW: Are there Irish cheeses that are used, for instance, in Les Halles?

AB: We're a French restaurant.

TW: Do you come across Irish cheeses in New York?

AB: A few, yeah, more and more.

TW: Which ones?

AB: Eh . . . What's that blue . . . Had it today, a really fine blue cheese?

TW: OK.

AB: Completely escapes me . . . I should point out that there are great Irish cooks. Nothing new about that.

TW: So who are the great Irish cooks of the past that spring to mind?

AB: No great . . . there are not many Irish celebrity chefs, but people who have been doing real cooking, you know, without being celebrated, which is to say, like most of the great cooks over the decades in this century, many, many, *many* Irish . . . and increasingly, you know . . . Conrad . . . ?

TW: Gallagher.

AB: Yeah. All right, he left New York in handcuffs, but . . . *(laughs)* He is not unique. A lot of chefs spend some time in handcuffs at some point or another!

TW: Does a restaurant critic need to know how to cook?

AB: No, I don't think so. They should know how to eat and enjoy the experience. They shouldn't be angry walking in the door.

TW: Dinner tonight: would you prefer to have it in London or New York?

AB: Wow, that's a hard question. OK, I think there are more great restaurants in New York, without question, and much more variety, particularly when you're talking about ethnic food. We have so many more foods from different cultures. But on this particular night and most nights I would rather eat at St. John restaurant in Clerkenwell.

TW: Henderson [the owner] hasn't been in the kitchen for a year . . .

AB: Well, he can't, but look, he's a visionary. He's a state of mind. He is a rightly influential leader of men and women and . . . God, I love that restaurant . . . I love Gordon Ramsay's restaurant also . . .

TW: What about restaurant criticism. Is there a healthier scene in New York or London?

AB: Hmm, I don't know. I mean, I think the *Times,* the *New York Times,* tries to set an industry standard and do very well at it, unlike most restaurant critics elsewhere. I don't really know the situation in London . . . I've read a lot of these guys, I mean . . .

TW: What about in terms of the competition? Which is more vibrant?

AB: I'm a huge admirer of Adrian Gill's column. Is that restaurant criticism, really? I mean, I don't think so. I know him and I like him. I'm sure I would be *horribly* wounded if he gave me a trashing! I saw one column of his, a restaurant review, and the first two . . . the entire article was about the phenomenon of anal seepage, with the final involuntary anal seepage *(laughs)* . . . It was hilarious and enjoyable, but is it criticism? I think the difference between a lot of restaurant criticism elsewhere and the *New York Times* is the *New York Times* tries very hard to send their critic in anonymously, in disguise, using a variety of aliases, different credit cards. They eat four or five times in the restaurant.

TW: Does that necessarily make the critic a better judge?

AB: I think it's more fair. I think they can still get it dead wrong, but I think that when you're talking . . . they have so much influence on the public. They can make or break a restaurant. You know, millions of dollars are at stake, and I admire the fact that they make every effort to be fair, to give you every chance. If you had a bad night, they will come back. They won't make or break you based on one experience, which I think is dreadfully unfair. If your paper can afford . . .

TW: Those are the rules of democracy, right? That when you pay, you enter into a contract. Surely you have a right to expect a certain level of . . .

AB: But you walk in the door, too, hoping to choose from a large menu. As a food critic, you go in . . . how many things can you try without tipping your hand, to start with, in which case you're probably getting special service? You know, I think it is fair, at least, to try to visit as many times as possible and choose as many things as possible. It can only be for the good. I do think, you can still gain very valuable information from just walking in cold, just giving it one shot and telling us about it. That's what I do all the time in writing about food and I don't think that's unfair or not valuable.

TW: But if you dress up a few times, that necessarily makes your opinion a little bit more fair?

AB: I think if you're the *New York Times* and you can carry a big stick like that . . .

TW: So it's the fact that you work for the *New York Times*?

AB: When you're that important to the success or failure of restaurants, rightly or wrongly, just by virtue of this is the big dog in town — I think it is the fairer of the two. Does that mean you get a better or more valuable review? Not necessarily. I mean, these guys have been wrong a number of times. A lot.

TW: What about objectivity?

AB: I'm talking here, the *Times,* they go in anonymously. They are very personal; the end product is a very personal view. They talk about their own preferences, their likes and dislikes and their subjective experience. I think more so lately, and I think that's to their credit.

TW: But again, if they're going to be personal, does it really matter whether they go back once, twice or ten times?

AB: You just get a wider range of experience, more to talk about, hopefully. A little more knowledge can never hurt.

TW: Or we're introducing more of their prejudices?

AB: And that happens, sure. What enrages me is the Zagat guide, because here you've supposedly got this impartially collected data that's collated, followed by three or four deadly sentences decided by who, I don't know, and you get these ridiculous things like this takeout soup joint in New York after twenty years getting the same rating as Le Bernardin. I mean, that's ridiculous.

TW: What about Paris? Is Michelin finished?

AB: I think the Michelin three stars are in real trouble. They're on the decline, and everyone seems to know that in Paris, too.

TW: And what about Michelin, in terms of its credibility? Have you read Pascal Rémy's book, for instance?

AB: Uh, no. I've heard about it. I don't know. I guess there's always a place for it [Michelin]. You know, it's just like Zagat: it's good because you know the name and the address, the phone number. That's useful. I don't think it is the be all and end all that it's meant to be, and I don't think it should be, and I think, in fact, it's their criteria that's so deadly.★ Because who could afford to run a three-star restaurant anymore? You can't! And who wants to eat in one anymore? It's certainly that kind of slick formal regime. You see these smart three-star chefs very shrewdly looking to create more informal, accessible, and fun dining experiences. You know, Robuchon's doing the Atelier thing, Ducasse has been opening these less fun, death-knell downscale versions . . . you know, if you look at guys who do that level of food really well — Thomas Keller, Napa Valley, Ferrán Adriá in El Bulli — those are fairly

---

★Of the four restaurants awarded three stars in Michelin's first New York guide, three are French, and each is run by a chef once fêted in *America's Elite 1,000*. That is not a salute. In the 2006 Zagat survey, the words "as good as Michelin" are no longer printed on the back cover. No matter; neither Zagat nor Michelin quite does it for me in Manhattan. I want to find someone who bridges a gap between "God-awful solipsism" and "outsize wig collection."

inexpensive restaurants, and it's fun to eat there. The level of service, well, it's resting in the efficient and traditional, yet still it's
friendly. They constantly try to delight you. They want you to
laugh and have a good time, and eat with your hands and rub
bread around in sauce. It's not like . . . I ate at Alain Ducasse New
York a few times. It was just this unendurably full-of-itself, formal,
unpleasant, intimidating and demanding experience. You feel like
a hoodlum for putting your elbows on the table. What fun is that?

TW: I read an interview in which you talk about how it's your responsibility to make wise decisions about where and what to eat,
taking the onus away from food producers.

AB: Right.

TW: Don't McDonald's say that?

AB: Yeah, but who are they kidding, you know? It's McDonald's!

TW: But it's the same rationale, isn't it?

AB: Uh, no. I mean, I think if you live well . . . *(pause)* I mean, I
hate to agree with McDonald's for anything, but I think if you
pour McDonald's burning hot coffee on your genitals, it's kind of
silly to sue them. If you look around at any major American city
or anywhere, there's that swath of destruction that McDonald's
has created across the world, leaving fat, unhealthy people behind.
Yeah, I think you're on your own. I think, yeah, if you're dumb-
ass enough to be eating McDonald's every day, don't go crying to
them later if you're fat and your heart's clogged. I think you
should take personal responsibility.

TW: So there is no obligation on the part of food producers to
create food that is not going to kill their customers?

AB: *(long pause)* No, I think they should fulfill whatever reasonable
expectation — *reasonable* expectation — of hygiene, of safety, but

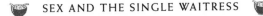

I think this is really dangerous ground here. The pendulum swings. The idea of absolute cleanliness, guaranteed cleanliness and absolute safety in every case, and absolute freedom from offense, or cruelty anywhere down the line, or long-term, as-yet-unanticipated effects . . . I just think, what in life can or should offer you that kind of guarantee? If you eliminate all risk . . . you eliminate all pleasure.

TW: OK, but there is a middle ground here between personal responsibility and the very real damage that some food companies are doing. Do you think government or food producers should be doing more to improve the food that we eat?

AB: No. I think it should be a chef-led and a consumer-led revolution.

TW: But again, with respect, that idea of a consumer-led revolution is very attractive, but it doesn't actually work. McDonald's is still the most popular restaurant in the world.

AB: McDonald's is popular because they have successfully taken advantage of lowered expectations. They successfully promise you what is essentially a fairly mediocre product, but the same mediocre product, consistently safe and consistently mediocre. It's the same mediocre hamburger, no less mediocre than the hamburger you had the day before, or the week before or that you had in another city or another country. It's convenient and it's consistent. It's not good; that's not what they're selling. That's not what their focus is.

TW: But you would accept . . .

AB: They're giving you the product they tell you. Where I draw the line is, back in the famous case in America where the judge threw out the "it's making me fat" [case], he said, "Well, there's no grounds for this, but it's very interesting . . ." He pointed out that the Chicken McNugget question is a little different. Now they tell you it is a *chicken* McNugget, but there's so much stuff in there that is not in fact chicken. You might have a case based on the argument that it is a deceptive product. The consumer should have a reasonable expectation that if something is called chicken, that it is within the bounds of reasonable expectations, not only for what it contains, but its effects on you. You know, there's a reasonable expectation to believe that chicken doesn't have a gazillion calories, or they spray it, you know, with beef flavoring. So you know, I can see, if you have rodent parts in your, in something you're selling me, I guess I would like to know.

TW: So you *would* be pleased if the government were to intervene on your behalf to ensure that some things are not . . .

AB: I think you're already way over-regulated. They're messing with my cheese; they're ruining my cheese. Look at these bastards, what they've done, you know? And look at those great thinkers — Arnold Schwarzenegger and Paul McCartney have made it illegal to sell, even *sell,* foie gras in California. This is not a good thing.

TW: OK, let's move on . . .

AB: One more thing. I think a perfect example . . . In a perfect world, you know, you walk down a back street in Mexico, you see a guy, a street vendor, not a very clean-looking food stall, but there are a lot of Mexicans there and they're rolling up quickie tacos off of a room-temperature pig's head with some very good-looking green sauce. It looks good, it smells good from your personal experience, the locals seem to like it. You make the calculated decision, "Well, it might make me sick, but it looks good . . ." You eat it. You pay, you play.

TW: OK, that's a point well made. *(pause)* You say you like A. A. Gill. I just want to return to him for a minute because he's kind of emblematic. He says that if food is all you care about, that doesn't say much for your company. Do you agree with that?

AB: I don't think he agrees with that. I don't think he believes that. He would like nothing more than if you were sitting in the bush in Africa eating bush meat with a local.

TW: But surely that proves his point? The context is often as important . . .

AB: I think Gill is very much like Ferrán Adriá. He's falling under this "don't try this at home, kids" department, meaning there's room in every country for maybe one Adrian Gill, and maybe in the world for one, OK, let's say two or three, Ferrán Adriás. Now Ferrán Adriá I think is a great chef, and I think he's influenced in a positive way a number of other chefs, a few, but unfortunately his influence has also had a very destructive effect on a lot of chefs who just aren't talented enough or inspired enough or intelligent enough to apply what they've experienced at El Bulli or read in his book in a positive way.

TW: OK, penultimate question. *(pause)* Well, not quite . . .

AB: *(laughing)* That's fine, I'm enjoying this.

TW: Sort of an ethical issue. How can anyone justify spending hundreds of dollars on one dish when millions of people are going to go hungry tonight?

AB: What's better? If you have the money or can get the money, in the range of silly things, which is better, a thousand–dollar Prada bag, or a meal you will remember forever? Courtside seats at a Knicks game, or an expensive sports event?

TW: Right, no one ever complains about someone else spending exorbitant sums on tickets for a Knicks game . . .

AB: Or Manolos?

TW: Yeah, or Manolos.

AB: I think, when I had no money, I would max out my credit card. I would squander money I could not afford once a year to go eat at Lutèce in New York. It affected my whole life; it made my whole year. It was timeless; I'll always remember it. Whereas the expensive jacket I bought in 1972 for the same price — where is that now?

TW: But again, the fact that someone is even in a position to spend so much money in an expensive restaurant when millions of people simply will not eat tonight . . . you've got to accept that there's something disturbing about . . .

AB: Sure, but there's something disturbing about every time we wake up having more privileged lives. Our entire existence, the language we speak, the clothes we wear, where we are this second, built on a mountain of human skulls maintained by the sweat and toil of people we've never met who will be beaten and flogged to death so that we can breathe this air. I think to realize that, understand and feel bad about it, and do something about it if possible, is entirely appropriate, and a good thing. All I can say to that is I eat a lot of expensive meals, but I also travel a lot, and I see the people we're talking about, and I don't know whether I do any good in the world, but I'm not afraid to see it first-hand, and to learn. It's not an intellectual argument for me. I have been in, in many ways even worse . . . I have allowed desperately poor people in Cambodia to feed me, to welcome me into their homes, a privileged guy, and share their meals with me and it's one of the greatest experiences of my life. *(pause)* You know, I don't know . . . I don't think . . . *(pause)* It's a tough question. I mean, I think knowledge, pleasure, experience, compassion, are all of a part. I guess it sounds facile to say, well, if I thought that by forsaking my cup of fettuccine tomorrow this would help someone, that I would. I don't know. I think that, again, every person has to look in their hearts and make, you know, that kind of judgment and decision about their own behavior.

TW: Do you think it's strange that people who work in this business so rarely consider the ethical dimension, that question that I've just asked you?

AB: It's funny, because so many chefs come from relative poverty. It's a blue-collar profession. In fact, a lot of chefs are very involved in the social problems to do with hunger and agriculture. As Raymond Blanc — who runs a very swank place — says, why does he cook so well? "Because I am a peasant, I grew up part . . ." You know, from a generation of peasants.

TW: But it *is* strange, isn't it?

AB: The question never comes up because my priority as a chef, as a sensualist, as a self-indulgent guy but mostly as a chef, my obligation is, *is it good*? Does it please me and does it please my customers? I don't care if it's genetically manipulated if it is better than a non-GM product. I don't care if it's organic or not; if this tomato is better than the organic one, then fuck the organic one. I care to some extent — it's a value judgment I make on the road all the time. Will I eat it? If I am offered bear bile . . .

TW: What's that?

AB: Bear *bile*. Incredibly cruel. They leech it out of bears. They think it's the greatest thing ever for your health. As an honored guest in Vietnam and Cambodia, I'm often approached by my smiling host: "Look what I got for you!" Now, I can offend my host, who will look at me like I've got two heads if I turn down something that's so good, or I can smile and take it. All the time. (*pause*) OK, shark fin. I'm never going to go looking for it, but I'll find myself at a Chinese banquet and they'll say, "Look what we have for you" — I'm going to eat it. There is a line, but it's an arbitrary one. *Live monkey brain.* I'm not going to do it. Why? I just decided that any expectations of how good it might be — the argument that it might be good, or that I might offend somebody if I don't eat it, is overwhelmed by it just being fucking horrible and cruel. *Dog and cat.* I've made a deliberate effort in my travels to not find myself in the position where I'm offered them. But I'll tell you, if you are a poor and proud Southeast Asian and I'm in your home, lying on your floors, I've met your kids, I've seen how you live — when you're that involved and they come at you with a tray of steamed puppy heads, I now have a choice between violating my completely arbitrary overvaluation of a cute animal and offending my host. I like to think that, well, sorry Fido.

TW: OK. What positive role, if any, do restaurants play within a society?

AB: Well, in much the same way as the coffee house was seen as a dangerous social element to the aristocracy because [that's where] people met and talked, it's very useful. It's a place where ideas and expectations about food and culture . . . It's a stage for ideas, for important things. Pleasure and food is good. Alcohol is good. Foreign influence is *very* good. When you look at how much better the world is since sushi became big, since good Chinese food started popping up everywhere . . . it creates appetites and interests beyond our tiny little lives.

TW: OK. Finally, I'm writing a book called *Kitchen Con*. Do you mind, and, if not, what advice would you give me?

AB: Well, I'm hardly in a position to object. Why not? It's a good title. As far as advice, have you seen *Jamie Confidential,* the cover of it? It's an unauthorized biography of Jamie Oliver, and it's exactly the same cover as *Kitchen Confidential* — the same text, the same layout . . .

TW: Oh, yeah?

AB: You know what? Try putting some sex every forty-eight pages.

15

The Critic on Trial: Part I

The Prosecution

I THOUGHT KITCHEN CON WAS A TERM THAT MIGHT DESCRIBE THE behavior of a cartel: *la cuisine des criminels*, in which chefs masquerade as maestros, or simply pinch their recipes; the twilight robbery of restaurateurs; and the con at its purest as practiced by critics, How to Eat Everything for Nothing. In writing this book, I have learned that ignorance is no excuse. That makes me the Kitchen Con, and this a book of evidence. Let the charge sheet record that even my thesis was borrowed without permission, from a man, Dr. Johnson, who never once sought to champion the philistine.

Prosecute me for a range of sins, but don't forget the coaccused. A critic has the temerity to share his opinions on the national stage, and the cheek to say nothing about his favorites for fear that the masses will descend. He is even more suspicious than most strangers, because he is both a player and a loudmouth. It is natural to doubt his credentials. Hence a pleasure for anyone reading a restaurant review is to unravel the connection, agenda, or preconception that handicaps the writer. We devour reviews in the hope of exposing critics — and with good reason, for they are just as small-minded, resentful, and wicked as everyone else. A city's complement may be no wiser than, say, your

189

average football team, and even more debauched. If they have a moral compass, it is clearly heading south. Alone or in groups, they drink too much and think nothing of resting on guests. (When a critic takes you out to dinner, borrows your pen, flirts with your wife, and asks you to drive him home, you must understand that these are elements within a greater ritual. Eventually, he will commit the meal to print, in a review that flatters your wife and slates the meal. The pity of it all is that this was your favorite restaurant. And you live beside the chef.) It is not solemn respect for the duty of a judge that informs the daily journey. It is hunger, the father of greed.

That skepticism is not misplaced. All writers are prostitutes, as Lenny Bruce said, and there are numerous grounds for believing that critics should be locked up. I have learned the truth of the words that open *The Journalist and the Murderer,* a meditation on media ethics by Janet Malcolm: "Every journalist who is not too stupid or too full of himself to notice what is going on knows that what he does is morally indefensible. He is a kind of confidence man, preying on people's vanity, ignorance or loneliness."

Journalists take delight in exposing bad behavior. They often combine it with a disregard for ethics in their own work. Jamie Oliver, Conrad Gallagher, Gordon Ramsay, and Nigella Lawson have all complained about interviewers who were unfair, insincere, or biased. It is normal, apparently, to assess hotels by paraphrasing press releases. Kola Boof says she was never a prostitute, contrary to a claim in the *New York Times.* "That story greatly hurt my life," she told me, "and there has never been any justice for me in the matter."

Consider, then, the preface to my conversation with Tony Bourdain. It may have informed your reading, but that introduction also prejudiced it. It was disingenuous to spend so much time outlining the context — *my* context — before asking you to read the interview verbatim. I gave the famous chef no leeway. Would he have seemed wittier or more incisive if I had picked some quotations and scattered them throughout the book? Reviewing the British edition of *Kitchen*

Con, one critic claimed that running the interview in full was an obvious way to beef up the word count. Was it? I could have shafted Bourdain by running stray remarks out of context. I could also have made him appear more cogent. Would it have been fairer to run selected passages? And fairer to whom? The reader, the subject, and the interviewer each has a different agenda.

Bourdain trotted out tales about the food he ate for a TV show. What does that suggest about his attitude to the media? The more he repeated his crazy stories, the more conventional he appeared. It was opportunistic to plug a mate (he had just written an introduction to Fergus Henderson's book), but Bourdain made incisive, amusing remarks about many of the subjects discussed in this book. I also thought that by reading the transcript, you, like me, would appreciate his answer to the final question. When Tony Bourdain told me to put some sex in the errant child of *Kitchen Confidential* — once every forty-eight pages — I thought he proved himself a *mensch.*

One long interview, so much unsaid. Consider, then, the silent mass of criticism. Journalists always say that bad restaurants go bust all by themselves. Bullshit. Sixty professionals can lose their jobs on the strength of one bad review. A man can take his own life.

The first chef to list his company on the Paris stock market, Bernard Loiseau, had a hotel beside Burgundy's vineyards, three Michelin stars, a host of imitators, a line of frozen foods, and even a boutique. Amid troubles in the stock market and rumors that Michelin was about to remove a star, Loiseau dropped a couple of points in the *GaultMillau* guide. These remarks are from the review in its 2003 edition:

> When Bernard Loiseau forces his smile on the cameras, hammering each syllable like he's driving in a stake, his desire to seduce seems accompanied by a subliminal fear that he is not succeeding. Today, we will write what everyone more or less knows: that this cuisine is not exactly dazzling, but simply very well done and pleasant.

Loiseau warned a friend that he would commit suicide if he lost one of his Michelin stars, and the *GaultMillau* review was a harbinger. A few days later, the chef went up to his bedroom, told his son to go into the garden, picked up a gun that had been a present from his wife, and shot himself.

Loiseau's suicide provoked a backlash against restaurant reviewers. "They are eunuchs," said Paul Bocuse, plagiarizing Brendan Behan, "because they know how to [cook] but they cannot do it." Many chefs joined the chorus, revealing the power, or lunacy, of the guides, and in the opinion columns of our own newspapers, journalists took critics to task. How could we do so much damage?

Bernard Loiseau was not killed by Michelin. He killed himself. The chef was obsessed with his reputation, and for him that meant all those stars. His death was a warning to those who would speak too glibly, perhaps, but not without sincerity. In killing himself, Loiseau was calling into question the morality of all criticism, and, worse, scaring off truth. A dishonest critic is no more useful to a society than a corrupt politician or a pedophile priest. Posing as a friend of the people, each abuses his position. It is possible, then, to depict the death of Bernard Loiseau as merely a waste of talent. But even that seems self-serving. No chef ever said that a bad review was good for his health.

All reviews are troubling in at least one sense. When Ruth Reichl told her housemates on a commune about her new career, they said, "You're going to spend your life telling spoiled, rich people where to eat too much obscene food?" Critics encourage readers, however inadvertently, to eat rich food and to drink a lot of wine.* In marketing

---

*A friend owns a chain of fashionable bars. When he is being particularly smug, I introduce him to strangers as an upmarket drug dealer. Bit rich. Journalists are forever glamorizing the psychiatric illness of addiction. Look at the way Pete Doherty is lauded as a romantic hero; the man is unwell. What does that make his sycophants in the press? Restaurant critics are enthusiastic champions of drug abuse. They seldom mention drunk driving, and never see fit to note that nearly half of all hospital admissions are alcohol-related or that each Briton drinks the equivalent of twenty-eight bottles of vodka every year. Such statistics have no place in the annals of restaurant criticism.

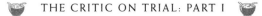

conspicuous consumption, it might also be argued that there is no difference between a good review and an advertisement for Dunkin' Donuts. Yet, despite our preaching, few discuss restaurant culture as an arm of a larger industry. Big Food demands attention: most critics could not be more blasé about that fact. Finally, when an entire industry conspires, as it did, to ignore the danger that BSE poses to humans, critics may represent a threat to the welfare of all their readers. Is there a moral distinction between this negligence and lying about weapons of mass destruction?

"Come on," say critics, "you can't blame us for society's problems. We have never pretended to have all the answers."

Oh, but you have.

In a west of Ireland pub, after ten years doling out answers, I started to ask some questions. Simon Wright was the editor of the *AA Restaurant Guide* until 2002, when he resigned in protest over the rating, in his own guide, of Petrus (Wright's boss had tried and failed to reserve a particular table at the restaurant for an important lunch). In his book *Tough Cookies,* which was written around the time I went to Roundstone, Wright reveals the bankruptcy of his own judging system:

> There are maybe 40,000 restaurants in the UK and even the biggest inspection teams number fewer than 30 people. That means only a small proportion of the total number is ever visited by any guide and those will mostly be the same ones in each book because all the guides feed off each other's information. Then consider that most of these restaurants will get only one visit in a twelve-month period, which makes the inspection nothing more than a snapshot — things occasionally go wrong in every kitchen. And then there's the question of the whole criteria for a rating. Yes, we can try and assess the quality of the produce, the accuracy of the cooking, the intelligence of the flavour combinations, but in the end it is a constant struggle to make a subjective assessment as objective as possible and to get a group of very different individual inspectors to look for exactly the same things in wildly different styles of food.

Simon Wright concludes that readers should not take reviews too seriously, as they provide no more than a general indication: this restaurant is good, that restaurant is bad. Wright is on to something here, but does he go far enough? There is only one Don King in the boxing business. That grizzly old bluffer is loudmouthed, boorish, always looking for a fight. Is the restaurant racket full of Don Kings? There is something suspicious about a mode of writing that simultaneously purports to be overview, prediction, research, and judgment. No critic claims that his view is truly comprehensive, yet in the act of writing a review each pretends that his opinion is in some way authoritative. You will never read a critique that starts with the words, "I might be wrong, but . . ." Even the most frivolous bar review in a supermarket tabloid is presented as fact, rather than the hung-over musings of a trainee alcoholic. This is laughable, and it is prudent to remember as much.

To be completely sincere about this whole business, let us admit that all reviews should be prefaced with a stern admission: no man can truly predict what sort of experience another is going to have in a restaurant. Our meals are various, which often has less to do with chef than mother, lover, husband. When the British journalist Kathryn Flett was sent on a junket to Bruges for the weekend, she gamely reviewed a roulade of ray with a cherry beer sauce and a heady Médoc, before succumbing to public tears:

> With the coffee came more tears, more stoicism. The carefully cultivated atmosphere of "romance" was proving difficult because, obviously, [my husband and I] were here to sift and scavenge through the detritus of romance, not feast on it. We were the last to leave the restaurant, and our marriage summit resumed in Suite 50 and went on until about dawn before it faltered and was abandoned . . . If your marriage has to end, perhaps it is better that it does so against the backdrop of a city like Bruges, rather than under the sodium glare of a streetlamp outside the local chip shop or on the sofa in front of the nine o'clock news.

In choosing to publish such a faithful account of her Belgian weekend, Kathryn Flett produced a fine piece of journalism. But the experience itself was not so unusual. Something similar happened to me in Prague, in exactly the same circumstances. One of the things that makes criticism so ludicrous is the implication that real life is somehow irrelevant to one's experience of a restaurant. I half-expected to meet Osama Bin Laden in the lobby of a small hotel. I *always* expect to meet Kevin Kelly. If mother is coming down off Prozac and father has a hangover, will you enjoy your dinner? What of the first glimpse of the boss and someone else's wife, caught in a clinch that will later be discussed at the water cooler? Do you remember what you ate that day? And were you hungry? A man who has not eaten for twenty-four hours is a different animal to the critic enjoying his third great meal of the day.★

I don't know if the chef is losing his religion, his job, or his mind. I cannot really say if the maître d' is on the tabloid payroll. How can I tell if he's more concerned with famous tits than finding me a seat? And why not? Perhaps the poor man will contract meningitis between the time he snubs my breasts and the day I slate his manners. How can I predict that he will irritate you when he might simply hate the sight of me?

The implication that another person can describe what your meal is going to be like on the basis of their experience is no more rational than announcing your horoscope, which is also full of pompous fictions. When you see a restaurant review and the astrology column on the same

---

★Nonsmokers claim to have a more sensitive palate than smokers. There is one vice that certainly dulls the palate.

HOSTESS: I'm afraid your table's not quite ready. Would you like a drink at the bar?

EMINENT GOURMET: Only if you think that it's absolutely necessary to get hammered before we eat.

HOSTESS: Oh, no, that's not what I meant at all.

EMINENT GOURMET: Fine. We'll go straight to the table, and mine's a pint of gin.

page of a newspaper, you know that the editor has a sense of humor. They are two great rackets, and the public can't get enough of them.

Paul Bocuse was wrong. Restaurant critics are not like eunuchs. I was wrong, too, when I compared them to hookers, the original ladies who lunge. That was unfair to chefs. Critics — even great critics — are like very bad lovers. They only come once a year, they don't care if you're not ready, they leave without saying a word, and then they tell everyone what you did wrong.

Doesn't that sound like the sort of person who deserves to be locked up?

16

The Critic on Trial: Part II

The Defense

THE APPETITE HAS A HABIT OF REVIVING ITSELF. IF WE ARE SLAVES, it is to the smell of strong coffee in the morning. We make of such forces what we will, in ways more numerous than the lies we daily tell ourselves. Some people concentrate on the avoidance of misery; others dedicate themselves to the pursuit of happiness. Some people believe in God; a lot trust gold alone. One or two starve themselves to death, while others become some sort of addict. Like suicide bombers, they take everyone else out too.

Becoming a critic is another one of the ways we respond to appetite: "a disinterested endeavour," in the famous words of the cultural critic Matthew Arnold, "to learn and propagate the best that is known and thought in the world." That definition was more relevant to nineteenth-century literature than it is to a dining room in the twenty-first century. It reeks of the ivory tower, and the restaurant itself is now a more egalitarian place than it has been at any time since the French Revolution. That a small number of us can finally afford to dine well and in some style is a remarkable development. Let us not ruin that privilege by ignoring the spectacular pleasure that people derive from eating out.

A secular mantra: "Create all the happiness you are able to create; remove all the misery you are able to remove." If those are noble aims, then restaurants are important sources of welcome, wonder, and warmth. The best play a valuable role within a society. So do critics. You need the food cops, no matter how pompous or ignorant we appear. Don't lock us up.

I defend that view, and thus myself, with reference, first, to statistics, and then to events in my week, every week.

Over two-thirds of American teenagers feel stressed at least once a week. (Poor things. They watch an average of twelve hours of television every week.) In newspapers, the use of terms like "self-esteem" and "trauma" rose exponentially in the 1990s. A 2005 report by the New Economics Foundation concluded: "Too much food has made the nation obese, more guns make our streets unsafe, excessive commercialism strips lives of real meaning."

Freud noted that humans oscillate between a need for security and a need for freedom. The author of *Willing Slaves,* Madeleine Bunting, argues that at some point in the last thirty years, "We pretty much junked security in favor of freedom. The price we pay for that is a kind of nervy, risk-taking, rollercoaster ride of adrenaline and depression. We've replaced lives that were nasty, brutish, and short with lives which are insecure, disorientated and long."

Religion and family are on the wane, and without the shared goals of a generation that grew up during a war, our lives have never seemed less important or more random. With all our new freedom, we turn to ersatz events like the climax of *Big Brother,* or — if that's not on — some local derby, in an effort to simulate a sense of achievement. We watch television programs about genocide that are interrupted by advertisements for car insurance. Our relationships are going fantastically well, until they suddenly disintegrate. Our jobs are a hoot, until we are fired.

"What lies behind the escalating weight of emotional distress," writes Bunting, "is that awful struggle to make meaning, that instinct that our lives should have a narrative and a purpose and should make some sense."

On the day he was sacked from his job, the writer James Atlas took his son to see the New York Rangers play at Madison Square Garden. Sitting in the best seats, Atlas tried to ignore the feeling in the pit of his stomach as he watched a bunch of professional athletes play out a drama that had nothing on his own afternoon. Later, he wrote, "What a bumpy ride. Were all lives like this? Was it a condition of existence that it never reached a plateau of even momentary equilibrium?"

"You know, I'm fifty-six," he says elsewhere, "but I feel twenty-six. I can't believe I go to meetings and I'm the oldest person there. And it's really hard for people to understand that everyone my age feels this way."

I cannot speak for James Atlas, though I also feel like half an adult. You may think it strange that I rarely cook. I have friends whose favorite dish is Wake and Bake. The twenties were supposed to last ten years. At times, I think youth and its attendant sexuality are the only game in town. That may be why my dentist has started to wear a baseball cap.

New media allow us to ingest more information than ever before, but that information is complemented less and less by personal experience. This applies even to people who lead lives that are, we assume, full of incident. Three days after being voted the best chef in the world, Heston Blumenthal was asked what he did in his spare time. The man whose molecular gastronomy has been called the most exciting development in culinary history paused. Might he be a fencer, or a black belt in karate? Does he climb mountains or go skydiving? Is he a poet, perhaps?

"My wife cooks the Sunday dinner," said Blumenthal, "and there is a riot if I miss that. Then on Monday it is the Indian takeaway and a DVD. You know how sad your life is when you know the release date of DVDs."

Stripped of meaning, life can feel like a series of incidents in which our role is clearly delineated: we are merely consumers. On bad days, I do not think of them as incidents at all, but as retail moments. That is a painful admission, and a shame, because status is not irrelevant. People who perceive themselves to be lower in the social hierarchy die younger than those just above them, and that applies at every level: Oscar winners die, on average, four years later than Oscar nominees.

I don't think life makes sense; most of the things we do are futile, and I am haunted by my own failings. Nothing unusual about that. Meritocracy encourages us to believe that we can have everything we want. Consumerism says we deserve it. If you haven't achieved all that you want to, the message of meritocracy is that you've messed up, and you don't deserve success. Consumerism encourages a similar conclusion: you've failed, and, what's worse, you've been cheated, because you deserve whatever you want.

I try to ignore advertising that promises an improvement in my status, as my self-esteem is quite low enough. And I am a bloody magazine editor. If there is value in my life, I think, on a good day, that it has less to do with my purchasing power than many of the messages I receive suggest. These are among the things I cherish: freshly squeezed orange juice, a game of tennis, good conversation, the fact that I can cycle to work, an opportunity there to influence opinion, the realization that I am very lucky.

It is comforting to create such a list, to pretend that there is an order to my life when there clearly isn't. Part of that pretense occurs on a Saturday morning. For one hour, I attend a meeting for the families and friends of drug addicts; here I am reminded that we are powerless over the actions of other people. This is bittersweet knowledge, but by the time I leave I am usually determined to take responsibility for my own actions. Then I walk across the city to a small French restaurant that doesn't accept reservations. It has a silly name, L'Gueuleton, which is French, apparently, for a gathering that turns into a party. Or something.

I do look forward to a cup of coffee.

The little French place, which is what everyone I know calls it, opens at half past twelve, and by that time I am usually around the corner, hungry and flagging. Ever since Tom Doorley wrote a rave review in the *Irish Times,* the restaurant has been packed, but because I arrive as it opens, and because I am a restaurant critic, I am offered a good table.

For two hours, I sit in the company of my girlfriend and one or two friends, reading the papers, discussing the events of the week, or diligently compiling lists of no importance.* It is understood that the meal *is* the event and the restaurant *is* the destination, not somewhere en route. There is no soundtrack, apart from the muted hum of conversation and the tender laughter of pals, lovers, family; a mother and her daughter, perhaps, comparing emotional scars. I like this laughter. It is less anxious and more intimate than midweek restaurant cackling. Hearing it suggests that the leisure industry does not yet have a monopoly on leisure.

---

*Some Things I Hate to Hear a Waitress Say

1. "Dad?"
2. "Welcome to the Hard Rock Café."
3. "What has she got that I haven't got?"
4. "I recommend the place . . . [whispering] next door."
5. "Who's the veal? Oh, I see. I thought you ordered the veal."
6. "To be fair, it does look like a fingernail."
7. "Jesus, I said I'm sorry. Give me a break; it's my first day."
8. "Look, I've already explained. Your card has been declined."

I study the menu and take some pleasure in not deciding what I want until the final moment. This false indecision feels, quite unreasonably, like a gesture of defiance. I usually start the meal with an avocado, bean, and chili soup and follow it with blanquette of lamb or a cassoulet of salt cod with mussels, haricots blancs, and prawn mayonnaise croûte. The food is always good. Succulent. Tasty. Delicious.

I surrender.

Looking around, I see many of the usual faces. Some of them come to this restaurant because it is fashionable to do so. They won't be here next week. Perhaps we will all move on to some new shrine in a few months. I don't think I will; at least, I hope not. This place feels familiar. I nod, half-smiling, once, at other congregants. Dublin is small enough to recognize strangers, and the few who live for a shot in the mouth, silent salvos in flavor, texture, contrast, often worship at the same address.

There is always some debate about whether we should have dessert. Then the waitress says what she says at this time every week. It is probably an insult. But the manner in which she says it is so benign and so familiar that I find it difficult to resist her invitation.

"Mr. White," she says, "why don't you let me choose?"

Ruth Reichl claims that we all become actors when we go out to eat. L'Gueuleton does feel like a small performance; occasionally, I become involved. There is a moment toward the end of the meal when the desire to consume is replaced by the urge to rise and leave the table. In the company of civilized people, we are taught, by our parents, or society, to ignore the urge. Each man has a remedy for such a plight. My own is sticky-toffee pudding.

"Happiness comes in small doses," says Denis Leary. "It's a cigarette, or a chocolate cookie, or a five-second orgasm. That's it, OK? You come, you eat the cookie, you smoke the butt, you go to sleep, you get up in the morning and go to fucking work, OK? *That is it.* End of fucking list. *'I'm just not happy.'* Shut the fuck up, all right?"

At last, that cup of coffee. No sugar, thank you.

If it is true that happiness comes in moments, then lunch on Saturday is a special reprieve, as it lasts somewhat longer than a man has a right to expect. Stolen verity in a day and a week and a life that is cellophane-wrapped yet full of small invasions, that dining room is a retreat — my retreat. I go for pleasure, as well as consolation. We each have such a place, and I don't think that we have ever needed it more.

Ditto critics.

As the number of choices in a marketplace increase, the negatives escalate until we become overloaded. At this point, choice no longer liberates us; it debilitates. One might even say that it begins to tyrannize. If you give shoppers the freedom to choose from half a dozen jams, they will select the one they like best. Offer them twenty and they will walk away confused, wanting jam, certainly, or not at all. Restaurant critics are not behind a movement to reshape retailing, and they have no great plan to rescue grace. There is good reason, as we have seen, to regard them with suspicion. But they serve at least one useful function.

The species leaves the kitchen, and now descends upon the dining room. We know why this is happening but have yet to acknowledge the implications. Lunch is fuel; succor, too. Most decisions about the quality of the food we eat are in the hands of strangers, which is why the matter deserves, or demands, some scrutiny. You *need* the food police to keep an eye on the antics of restaurateurs, chefs, and food producers. You *want* them to tell you where and what to eat.

Finally, if you think that people would be better off if they focused less on the pursuit of happiness, and more on the avoidance of misery, you may be right. Life may be a meaningless grind, as Woody Allen says. That doesn't change my conclusion. Eating out is among the best ways to avoid misery. Isolating those places in which one can expect a warm welcome, a little comfort, and a good lunch, critics play a vital role in the prevention of suffering.

Without grumblers in our midst, we would probably be dining off a rock.

17

Good Food, Good Life

On Demolishing the Bad

Good Food, Good Life

— Advertisement for Nestlé, Galway, March 2006

FTER TWO YEARS IN WHICH THE MAGAZINE CONSISTENTLY LOST
money, *The Dubliner* looked set to become a noble failure.
Then, in what truly felt like an act of desperation, we decided
to produce a compilation of our restaurant reviews. Kitchen-sink publishing. Eleven days later, the book became the best-selling restaurant
guide in Ireland, and in so doing it saved the business. This year, we
will publish the sixth edition. In 2005, a report in the *Sunday Times*
noted:

> *The Dubliner* [magazine] has grown to represent something en-
> nobling and affirmative. Its anthropological, ideas-driven mix
> does not quite belong to this century, or even the last, but owes a
> debt to the Victorian salon and to the explorer's pith helmet. It
> shouldn't have survived but it has, and so represents a welcome
> glimmer of hope.

More conventional tributes have been paid to the magazine, but that quotation comes closest to capturing the grand folly of the venture. We make more mischief than money — the function, perhaps, of a small, independent publication — and it feels like a privilege to provoke debate about subjects too long ignored.

But then, I would say that.

Journalists are good at creating narratives that misrepresent their role or status. I have done quite enough of that. So let me not pretend that the business is glamorous. That myth was created to impress advertisers. In publishing, as Rupert Murdoch noted, you make a lot of enemies. Competitors often print your obituary in order to steal your clients; those same clients are obsessed with the size of your circulation. Never mind the quantity, you say, feel the quality. But nobody listens. Even praise can be confusing. Readers say how much they admire the work of someone who writes for the competition.

There was a time when chefs were largely insulated from the sort of praise that publishers routinely receive. The Web has changed all that. Press a few buttons and suddenly one is grumbling for America. Thus it is possible to boil a cook in record time. On the face of it, this knowledge spells the end of food-writing as we know it — no more the nerdy clique of self-styled experts. Fine journalists have little to fear, however, as there will always be room for shrewd analysis and lively writing; what's changed is that so much of it is now found on the Internet. Hence blogs with culinary themes, like the recipes of Julia Child or the cooking in greasy spoons, are hailed as literary phenomena. (Meanwhile, angry waitresses exact revenge on lousy tippers by exposing them on bitterwaitress.com. Tom Cruise, Jennifer Lopez, Britney Spears, and Barry Manilow — his flan was "too caramelly" — all star on the site.)

The laws of media are changing, as millions of readers now participate in the creation of content in a way that has no historical precedent. Eventually — after it ends, no doubt — the tabloids will call it a revolution in reviewing. It may even result in a Golden Age for restaurants, as owners acknowledge that in order to win acclaim, *everyone* must be treated as a critic.

That departure marks a journey's end. In trying to voice a reservation, I have come to see the obsolescence of criticism, as well as its imprecision. As a restaurant reviewer, I share information and opinion with readers, but I do so in a way that is necessarily subjective. I could always claim to name the best tables, the worst wines, the must-come-back-again dishes, the cut of the owner's jib, the draught on table three, the size of the prawn cocktail, and the time it took to get the bill. Today, however, I don't say anything in print that I would not say to the subject's face, and I would not slate a place without good reason. The restaurant industry will often kill a man before it makes him rich. Insofar as I grew up, it was in the business, so I do have a duty of care. And I don't like custard pie. There is nothing unusual about this attitude, though it is, perhaps, more American than British.

Two hundred and fifty years ago, Dr. Johnson said nothing invented by man produces so much happiness as a good tavern or inn. I am the product of a culture that venerates futility; from Homer Simpson to Paris Hilton, we revel in the vacuous, the absurd, the self-mocking — in order, perhaps, to validate our own emptiness. Yet on occasion we also suspect that love may mean no harm, or even that man means well. In a good restaurant, we share a profound engagement with the natural world and with each other. There one eats, with pleasure and in style, among family or friends: the luminous few who lend some value to what we do. In such a place, our suspicions about love, and about each other, do not seem unreasonable. And in this symphony of basic needs met the dining room encourages us to presume, however briefly, that life itself means well.

So the restaurant is a source of inordinate happiness. In that knowledge, the work of the critic — "to make way for the good by demolishing the bad," as Kenneth Tynan put it — can seem ungrateful, or inelegant, at least. The regret is not, perhaps, that the journalist's tools are so crude, but that it's so hard not to hurt someone's feelings. "I'm not a consultant to the restaurant industry," writes A. A. Gill. "If they want a consultant, they can go out and hire one. Besides, you're dealing with real people's real money. You owe it to readers to be straight and tough." Being straight and tough is not always easy, as I discovered at the *Irish Times*. Gill is right, but so was the editor, an American, who once said, "It's OK to slap a man in the face, but you don't have to cut his cheek with your ring." Perhaps the challenge is to negotiate a path between the two positions.

In the kitchen, the country that gave us Spotted Dick and Blackpool Rock has been reborn. Its new life is evident in the dining room, and also on the pages of national newspapers, where food criticism has never been so popular. However, the emergence of a sophisticated restaurant scene in London, and the championing of that scene in the press, rather ignores the lingering smile of Ronald McDonald — and a gulf in the way that people eat. The average lunch break now lasts nineteen minutes, and in England, two-thirds of all meals eaten outside the home are curries. Elsewhere, hamburger chains are colonizing France, while legendary hosts like Soltner, Senderens, and Maccioni are rethinking or retrenching.

"If we had treated the young better," said Alain Ducasse recently, "they would not have switched to U.S.-style fast food. We have been obsessed with formality and unfriendly service. We have lost out to foreign restaurants as a result." It is certainly true that decorum and patience are necessary to appreciate the darlings of Michelin. Neither quality is found in abundance these days, and there is something faintly ridiculous about a lot of upscale/expensive restaurants, full of rich white neurotics on San Pellegrino. Never mind the menu, feel the nervous tension. There is no greater darling of Michelin, by the way, than Alain Ducasse, who has a grand total of nine stars. As Tony Bourdain said of his place in New York: "It was just this unendurably full-of-itself, formal, unpleasant, intimidating, and demanding experience. You feel like a hoodlum for putting your elbows on the table. What fun is that?"

In January 2007, Alain Ducasse closed the restaurant.

One should not ignore the food as one might overlook the elbows. Colin Tudge's eloquent defence of gourmet cooking makes the moral case for the sort of restaurants that Dr. Johnson would surely appreciate; and, in so doing, Tudge suggests that critics have obligations that dwarf the desire to chortle. Food is both cheaper and more plentiful than ever before, but the relentless drive for maximum profit has created manifold problems in its wake. Foot-and-mouth disease, vCJD, and genetically modified foods are all, in their way, a legacy of that determination. So is a food supply laced with outlandish quantities of sugars and fats. If we are serious about serving the public, critics have a responsibility to ask why restaurant chains, food producers, and supermarkets are marketing products that may do severe damage, either to their customers or to the environment, why millions of people are stabilized on a diet that is full of fatty, sugary, processed foods and why our governments are reluctant to tackle the issue.

When the politics of food production becomes headline news, restaurant critics will have questions to answer. So will chefs. Gordon Ramsay, that famous peddler of rarefied cooking, recently complained that organic food "has become hip and trendy, overhyped, overpriced, and inconsistent." In conclusion, said Ramsay, "there is now a snob factor attached to it." *Like haute cuisine is democratic.* You'd think a man who works in a kitchen would know the difference between a pot and a kettle. Then there's Tony Bourdain, who told me reluctantly that food companies "should fulfill whatever reasonable expectation of hygiene and safety," but he did so reluctantly. Bourdain didn't want to sound like a turkey voting for Christmas, because, as he put it, "if you eliminate all risk, you eliminate all pleasure." Chefs such as Bourdain promote the appreciation of good food as a local, seasonal privilege. It is understandable that they should oppose efforts to regulate the way that food is produced. But in doing so, they have inadvertently aligned themselves with enemies of good taste.

In the last four years, over twenty American states have enacted "common-sense consumption" laws that prevent customers suing large food and restaurant companies for making them fat and unhealthy. Those laws are the result of an aggressive campaign by organizations such as the National Restaurant Association, which represents everything from fast-food chains to culinary temples. They make uneasy bedfellows.

Professor Richard Daynard, one of the founders of the anti-tobacco movement, was recently asked to comment on the marketing of potentially unhealthy food. "People changed their minds," he said, "when documents started to come out about how tobacco companies misled customers about the alleged health benefits of light and low-tar cigarettes." Daynard predicts that fast food will suffer a similar fate: "People will start to realize that Ronald McDonald is not their friend."

In 2006, New York's health authority declared that the city is suffering from a diabetes epidemic. In California, where obesity cost businesses $21.7 billion in medical bills, workers' compensation, and lost productivity in the year 2004, junk food and sugary fizzy drinks have been banned from schools. The British government has promised to introduce a similar measure. And in April 2006, damning evidence of the correlation between obesity and fast food emerged, when a U.S. government report concluded that "the ready availability of inexpensive restaurants has not only caused people to consume more but has made them less active — less likely to prepare food at home or travel further distances to obtain a healthy meal." According to the authors of that report, the rapid increase in the number of restaurants per capita is the most significant environmental factor in America's obesity epidemic.

Finally, as I write, the latest news — apparently good — is that McDonald's has decided to invite customers to inspect its kitchens. The *Financial Times* comments:

> It is not quite the chef's table. Unlike expensive restaurants with famous cooks that charge a high price for customers to sit at a table near the kitchen and observe creativity at first hand, Mc-Donald's is allowing its patrons in for free. The U.S. fast-food chain wants to convince Europeans of the quality of its ingredients and cooking.

There is a pattern here — familiar, no doubt, to Morgan Spurlock. Inviting that comparison with the chef's table allows McDonald's to claim kinship with figures like Tony Bourdain, who told me that diners

should exercise more common sense about what they eat. Bourdain's objection to restrictions on the way that food is produced has nothing to do with market share; it is rooted in a love of food. In my giddy advertisement of the fact that dining out is more, much more, than food alone, I too became a useful idiot. And by peddling the cliché that critics and cooks are enemies, I failed to see them as allies in a greater battle. That was another mistake. Critics and cooks have much in common — more, certainly, than any real chef has in common with Ronald McDonald — and more to discuss than I once thought. At stake is the future of breakfast, lunch, and dinner.

Epilogue

Cashel Hill does not feature in the guidebooks. Not high enough to attract hillwalkers, too steep for a leisurely stroll, it is largely ignored by people who come to Connemara. Here, now, in the dead of winter, the sun rarely climbs above a man's shoulder, and it is hard to imagine that tourists ever find this awkward patch of bog and sky. This morning, I clambered to the summit with a local archaeologist. From there, we saw Clifden, the Maam Turks, Toombeola, and, away to the south, the Aran Islands.

"Do you see that port?" said the archaeologist, pointing at a row of buildings about five miles off to the west. "That's Roundstone."

We had lunch on a bench by the fire in O'Dowd's. I was tired but relieved that I had not slipped on the mud-soaked slope of the hill, so I ate with a sense of gratitude. Outside, fishing boats returned from their own expeditions, beating an ocean for pollock or plaice. There was no one else in the bar, and the owner started to tell us about the time that one of the Kennedys advised him to export his famous seafood chowder. It would, said the guest, do well in America. As I finished a second pint of Guinness and peered down at the empty bowl before me — replete, it seemed, in several ways — that seemed incontestable. No reason, indeed, to doubt that this was the greatest bowl of chowder in Ireland.

"You know," I said, "I should write about this."

But the archaeologist disagreed; neither plan, he thought, was sound.

"What class of fool," he asked, "would give that soup away?"

Returning, now, to the kitchen of the cottage that is temporary home, again — to conspire with Jamie Oliver. It is the only place where he will speak to me, and then only in the breathless patter of a celebrity cookbook author, encouraging the production of dishes like farfalle with a "quick" tomato sauce or North African lamb with chili, ginger, chickpeas, and couscous. Tonight, however, I am going to stick to something vaguely local, less ambitious: mushroom soup, roast chicken — organic, free-range — with parsley champ and buttered leeks. Sticky-toffee pudding, then, if I don't make a mess of everything else. Nothing comes quickly to the Kitchen Con, which makes repentance the more humbling.

In moments of reverie, frowning at the fridge or whisking something, I return to the diners who insisted on sitting beside the pass in a restaurant called Whites on the Green. I recall them cocking an ear for a sign that all is well, or proof that God is French. Before nouvelle cuisine became a synonym for small food at big prices, the term described a movement to use fresh ingredients in a way that was honest and to reduce the amount of processed food in the diet. Those are noble goals, the results just as interesting as the frantic efforts of a politician to seduce a waitress in diplomatic French. Twenty years later, I now begin to understand the thrill of sitting on table nine, just outside the kitchen. That's where the real action was.

Back, then, to the stove. There, one concludes that critics have the same intention. No matter how cruel or grave we appear, we are each on the side of pleasure. But don't get the wrong idea. I am not proposing some sort of reconciliation. That would be rather too gruesome for everyone.

No, this is an invitation.

The Twenty-First-Century Dining Room is quite big enough for the bookish cooks of earnest broadsheets, the pedigree chumps, and all the dogs of dinner. Head down, all smiles, there may be room for me, which means there *must* be a place for you.

Acknowledgments

I am very grateful to the following friends and colleagues for their assistance and encouragement: Sarah Ballard, Ed Brophy, Helen Lucy Burke, Niamh Cahill, Stuart Carolan, Declan Cashin, Conn Corrigan, Kate Dailey, Louise East, Anjuli Elias, Antony Farrell, Laura Farrell, Cilian Fennell, Alan Fitzpatrick, Joan Fitzpatrick, Sam Fitzpatrick, Sara Garvey, Patrick Geoghegan, Kathy Gilfillan, Gerry Godley, A. C. Grayling, Cian Hallinan, Eoin Higgins, Louise Higgins, Conor Horgan, Bridget Hourican, Cate Huguelet, Winter Hynes, Hugo Jellett, Sarah Jones, Beatrice Kelleher, Cormac Kinsella, Tim Macey, Danielle Malone, Max McGuinness, Cara Murphy, Tamara O'Connell, Aillil O'Reilly, Derek Owens, Carolyne Quinn, Vinnie Quinn, Valerie Ringrose Fitzsimons, Michael Ross, Robert Ryan, Sinead Ryan, Rosalind Sharpe, John Stephenson, Belle Taylor, Paul Trainer, Paolo Tullio, Camilla Van de Wiel, Rosie Waitt, and Tremain White.

Part of this book was written at the Tyrone Guthrie Centre in Annaghmakerrig, County Monaghan. Thank you to Sheila Pratschke. Thank you, also, to Sinead, Clodagh, Barbara, Billy, and Cavanagh Foyle at Dolphin Beach in Clifden. Blessed retreat.

My agent, Robert Kirby at Peters, Fraser and Dunlop, fostered the production of *Kitchen Con,* as did many of the team at Mainstream Publishing: Sharon Atherton, Graeme Blaikie, Emily Bland, Becky Pickard, Fiona Brownlee, Bill Campbell, Peter MacKenzie, and my editor, Kevin O'Brien. I am also grateful to my American publisher, Jeannette Seaver, and the wonderful Arcade team.

Finally, thank you to Audrey Ryan, for her patience and encouragement, and for being the victim of my own misdeeds in the kitchen.

Bibliography

Allen, Myrtle. *The Ballymaloe Cookbook*. Minneapolis: Irish Books, 1984.

Atkins, Robert C., M.D. *Dr. Atkins' New Diet Revolution*. New York: M. Evans, 2002.

Barnes, Julian. *The Pedant in the Kitchen*. London: Atlantic Books, 2003.

Blythman, Joanna. *Shopped: The Shocking Power of Britain's Supermarkets*. New York: HarperPerennial, 2005.

————*Bad Food Britain*. London: Fourth Estate, 2006.

Bourdain, Anthony. *Kitchen Confidential: Adventures in the Culinary Underbelly*. New York: Bloombsbury, 2000.

————*Les Halles Cookbook: Strategies, Recipes, and Techniques of Classic Bistro Cooking*. New York: Bloomsbury, 2004.

Brillat-Savarin, Jean Anthelme. *The Physiology of Taste*. New York: Counterpoint Press, 1999.

Bunting, Madeleine. *Willing Slaves: How the Overwork Culture Is Ruling Our Lives*. New York: HarperPerennial, 2004.

Chelminski, Rudolph. *The Perfectionist: Life and Death in Haute Cuisine*. New York: Gotham, 2005.

Conford, Philip. *The Origins of the Organic Movement*. Edinburgh: Floris, 2001.

Enzensberger, Hans Magnus. *Zig Zag: The Politics of Culture and Visa Versa*. New York: New Press, 1999.

Evans, Lloyd Thomas. *Feeding the Ten Billion: Plants and Population Growth*. New York: Cambridge University Press, 1998.

Fernandez-Armesto, Felipe. *Food: A History.* London: Macmillan, 2001.

Gray, John. *Straw Dogs: Thoughts on Humans and Other Animals.* New York: Granta, 2002.

Kelly, Ian. *Cooking for Kings: The Life of Antonin Carême, the First Celebrity Chef.* New York: Walker, 2004.

Kurlansky, Mark, ed. *Choice Cuts: A Selection of Food Writing from Around the World and Throughout History.* New York: Ballantine, 2002.

Lawrence, Felicity. *Not on the Label: What Really Goes into the Food on Your Plate.* New York: Penguin, 2004.

Levin, Bernard. *Enough Said.* London: Jonathan Cape, 1998.

Lloyd, John. *What the Media Are Doing to Our Politics.* London: Constable, 2004.

Malcolm, Janet. *The Journalist and the Murderer.* New York: Knopf, 1990.

Mallet, Gina. *Last Chance to Eat: The Fate of Taste in a Fast Food World.* New York: W. W. Norton, 2004.

Mondavi, Robert. *Harvests of Joy: How the Good Life Became Great Business.* New York: Harcourt, 1998.

Montagné, Prosper. *Larousse Gastronomique.* New York: Crown, 1970.

Orwell, George. *In Defence of English Cooking.* London: Penguin, 2005.

Pollan, Michael. *The Omnivore's Dilemma: A Natural History of Four Meals.* New York: Penguin, 2006.

Putman, Robert. *Bowling Alone: The Collapse and Revival of American Community.* New York: Simon & Schuster, 2000.

Rayner, Jay. *The Apologist: A Novel.* London: Atlantic Books, 2004.

Reichl, Ruth. *Garlic and Sapphires: The Secret Life of a Critic in Disguise.* New York: Penguin, 2005.

Rémy, Pascal. *L'Inspecteur se met à table.* Sainte-Marguerite sur Mer: Equateurs, 2004.

Richman, Alan. *Fork It Over: The Intrepid Adventures of a Professional Eater.* New York: HarperCollins, 2004.

Schlosser, Eric. *Fast Food Nation: What the All-American Meal Is Doing to the World*. New York: HarperPerennial, 2002.

Sheraton, Mimi. *Eating My Words: An Appetite for Life*. New York: Morrow, 2004.

Spencer, Colin. *British Food: An Extraordinary Thousand Years of History*. New York: Columbia University Press, 2003.

Steingarten, Jeffrey. *The Man Who Ate Everything*. New York: Knopf, 1997.

Strong, Sir Roy. *Feast: A History of Grand Eating*. New York: Harcourt, 2003.

Todhunter, Andrew, *A Meal Observed*. New York: Knopf, 2004.

Tudge, Colin. *So Shall We Reap: What's Gone Wrong with the World's Food — And How to Fix It*. New York: Penguin, 2004.

Visser, Margaret. *The Rituals of Dinner: The Origins, Evolution, Eccentricities, and the Meaning of Table Manners*. New York: Grove, 1991.

Watters, Ethan. *Urban Tribes: Are Friends the New Family?* New York: Bloomsbury, 2003.

Winner, Michael. *Winner's Dinners: The Good, the Bad, and the Unspeakable*. London: Robson Books, Limited, 2000.

Wright, Simon. *Tough Cookies: Tales of Obsession, Toil and Tenacity from Britain's Culinary Heavyweights*. London: Profile, 2005.

Young, Toby. *How to Lose Friends and Alienate People*. Cambridge, Mass.: Da Capo, 2003.

Index